NICK CATO

DARK DREAMS

An Obsessive Look at Romano Scavolini's NIGHTMARE

Headpress

A HEADPRESS BOOK
First published by Headpress in 2025, Oxford, United Kingdom
headoffice@headpress.com

DARK DREAMS
An Obsessive Look at Romano Scavolini's NIGHTMARE

Book & cover design : MARK CRITCHELL mark.critchell@gmail.com
With thanks to Gareth Wilson and Jennifer Wallis

10 9 8 7 6 5 4 3 2 ~~1~~

A CIP catalogue record for this book is available from the British Library

ISBN 978-1-915316-35-6 paperback
ISBN 978-1-915316-36-3 ebook
ISBN NO-ISBN hardback

TABLE OF CONTENTS

This one is dedicated to all the NIGHTMARE fans around the globe, especially those who cheered this project on and continually encouraged me.

For the late Rick Sullivan and Chas Balun: thanks for the advice, friendship, and early inspiration.

Hey Shannon: I love you.

AUTHOR'S NOTE

I began working on this book in early 2017. At that time, Code Red's DVD and Blu-ray editions of NIGHTMARE were the primary ways to see the film. While working on my manuscript, a couple of video companies announced they would be releasing yet another restored version of the film. Severin Films' three-disc set and novelization of the film were released in August 2023, as this book was in its final editing stages. It includes a new documentary about film distributor David Hamilton Grant. The chapter in this book that deals with Hamilton Grant was written in 2018–19, and doesn't draw on the documentary film for information.

In the DVD/Blu-ray chapter, I look at the three main American releases of the film. I am fully aware of the international versions (including the popular 88 Films edition from the UK) but have not covered them here, nor international releases. There is a plethora of reviews of discs online for those interested.

"In my film there is no hope,

because the real and final message is that

we are all at the mercy of our own demons."

—Romano Scavolini

INTRODUCTION

The first time I saw Romano Scavolini's 1981 film NIGHTMARE (also known as NIGHTMARES IN A DAMAGED BRAIN, BLOOD SPLASH, and a couple others mentioned in this book) was on a double bill with the equally insane MOTHER'S DAY (1980). I was a sophomore in high school, and it was either late 1982 or early 1983 when a few friends and I took the bus to a local theater in Staten Island, NY, after seeing it advertised in the newspaper. I remember drooling over both films' commercials on late night TV the years they were initially released, but I was still a bit too young to be admitted to either one. To say I was excited for this double feature is beyond an understatement.

While Charles Kaufman's film was (and remains) the more popular of the two, by the time Scavolini's feature unspooled its final reel, I simply couldn't get it out of my head. And yet my strongest memory of that night wasn't so much the film as it was the *reaction* of several

Ad for MOTHER'S DAY / NIGHTMARE double feature that ran in NYC newspapers, circa 1983.

patrons outside the theater afterwards. There were six people leaning against the front wall, discussing the gruesome images we had just witnessed during NIGHTMARE's infamous finale. Two of those people were teenage girls who were *collecting* themselves, questioning out loud what kind of people would make such a sick movie. It's safe to say both had regretted coming out to this debauched evening of horror cinema. I often wonder just how much these films, and especially NIGHTMARE, affected them and on what levels. Had they been turned off from seeing other horror films? Does the film still bother them to this day? I'll never know, but I'll assume in some way it does. I've never seen people react to a film like this before or since, and I've seen some truly disturbing films in the theater with full audiences.

Whatever you may think of the film today (even FX artist Ed French claimed he didn't think any of the gore scenes looked "very convincing"*), at the time, NIGHTMARE was as gory and disturbing as it could get, not to mention having its most violent murder committed by a child. The plot itself is a simple, generic slasher film trope (a dangerous psychotic is released prematurely from a mental institution) yet there is just something about the way Scavolini tells it that manages to get under your skin. Well, under *my* skin, and the skin of a dedicated legion of fans. The film is also loathed by many, was generally hated by critics, and its routine story has caused many within the horror community to dismiss it.

Chances are you're reading this because you, too, have been fascinated with this simple yet oddly effective film. Or perhaps you are of the camp who can't get past the (mostly) stiff acting, silly dialogue, gratuitous false jump scares, and one or two tedious scenes that manage to turn people off, especially in this modern age of impatient film viewing. Whatever your case, it isn't my objective to convince the reader NIGHTMARE is a great film, or that people are missing out on something the rest of us "get." This book is basically a tribute to a film that has refused to leave me alone. It has haunted me more than any other slasher film out there, including classics such as HALLOWEEN (1978), FRIDAY THE 13th (1980), and HENRY: PORTRAIT OF A SERIAL KILLER (1986). While each of the cited films are technically better than NIGHTMARE, and without question *scarier*, I'm hoping to be able, by the end of this book, to show just what it is that makes NIGHTMARE such an unforgettable experience. Although I've thought for well over 20 years it had to be the graphic gore sequences, it wasn't until my umpteenth viewing around 2010 when Code Red DVD released 30th and 35th anniversary DVD and Blu-ray editions that I had a change of mind. I hadn't seen the film for about 10 years before this, and upon my first revisit after that time the film's psychological aspect began to rear its ugly head to me. NIGHTMARE will always be known for its generous amount of blood shedding and sickening sound effects, yet I firmly believe most viewers are so taken aback by the kill scenes and technical issues that the head games it seeks to play with the audience are often lost. In my case, it was lost for over 20 years, in which time I had easily sat through

* Interview with FX artist Ed French on the 2011 Code Red DVD release of NIGHTMARE.

the film over 25 times, mostly on VHS and the one theatrical screening cited above. I've since seen it twice more in theatres (once in 2014 at a drive-in horror festival in Coxsackie NY, and most recently in 2017 in Brooklyn, NY at an Alamo Drafthouse film festival during a series dedicated to strange films shot in Florida). And for the sake of this book, I've lost track of my Blu-ray viewings.

I believe NIGHTMARE, while best known for its graphic gore sequences, is equally intense as a psychological chiller thanks in large part to actor Baird Stafford, who plays the schizophrenic George Tatum. He has little dialogue (in one sequence he apologizes to a victim in a regretful whisper), yet his facial expressions and mannerisms suggest someone who is truly, internally tormented. More so than most slasher film killers, Tatum is someone who could snap at any moment, and when we discover the reasons surrounding the gruesome double homicide he committed as a child, it's easy to sympathize with him as much as we hate ourselves for doing so.

Tatum is a man who has been revolted by sex from an early age. As an adult, he tries to help himself overcome his issues (an early scene in the film features him visiting peep shows in Times Square during its heyday) yet even simply seeing a topless woman begins to set back any help his stay at the institution may have had.

DON'T GO IN THE HOUSE and MANIAC (both 1980) are other fine examples of men internally tormented by women, as is HENRY: PORTRAIT OF A SERIAL KILLER (1986). Those who stood against slasher films during their explosion in the 1980s often pointed to their misogyny. The most famous horror film icons such as Jason Vorhees, Michael Myers, and Freddy Krueger often killed more women than men. Women were exploited in slasher films as producers knew it was the nudity and not just the violence that sold tickets. Yet despite its brief sexual content, NIGHTMARE isn't a misogynistic film. Unlike many horror film killers of the time, George Tatum wasn't bent on killing women because he "hated" them. His childhood experience of seeing his father tied to the bed as a woman slaps his face completely

2014: NIGHTMARE kicks off the first night of the annual DEAD 'TIL DAWN festival held at the Hi-Way Drive-In Theater in Coxsackie, NY (about 3 hours north of New York City).

distorted young George's mind toward sex (and whether that woman was a mistress or George's mom is still unclear after all these years. I further discuss this herein as part of two chapters). To George, *sex itself* is what must be punished, not the person doing it. In his childhood murder, George kills both people, not just the woman. As an adult prematurely released from a psychiatric ward, he quickly goes back to dispense his own twisted form of justice to members of both sexes (including his own children's babysitter *and* her boyfriend).

Which leads to another interesting aspect of the film: the fact that George Tatum was once married and had three children suggests the mental trauma he suffered as a child was somehow kept at bay during his teens and early adult years. The film doesn't tell us if he was given psychiatric counseling as a child, or if he was even caught for the murders. The adult psychiatrists in the film know he had an early traumatic experience, but not exactly what it was. Whatever the case, George, as an adult, somehow had a relapse that sent him to an institution in New York City for help. When he's prematurely released, he spends most of the film's running time traveling back to Daytona Beach, Florida, where his wife and children live. And along the way, to release his internal struggle, he randomly kills.

Perhaps the drive to kill his family developed out of a new awareness that he actually *had sex*, and that this personal sin must now be punished. Any fan of the film can fill in

their own reasons for his murder spree, but one thing is clear: George Tatum is *not* a misogynist. He's a damaged man who was taught about sex at an inappropriate age and that through witnessing his own father's unusual style *of it*. To say George Tatum is a typical horror film killer does the film a disservice, despite its generic slasher plot.

Mike Hunchback introduces NIGHTMARE for the "Weird Florida" film series, July 2017, at the Alamo Drafthouse, Brooklyn, NY.

INTRODUCTION

I've been obsessing over NIGHTMARE since the first time I saw it, and while this is no surreal arthouse film, it seems to offer things few other slasher films do. It's quite gory (at least for its time), but the psychological aspect I've just touched upon is only the tip of the ice pick. While Romano Scavolini himself ardently claims NIGHTMARE "isn't a slasher film"[*] (although *it is* even if it wasn't his intention), he has done something most films of its ilk don't and manage to *genuinely disturb the viewer*. Again, he does so on the surface with the gruesome kill sequences, but I believe it's our identification with George that manages to get under our skin. George was an everyday boy whose world was shattered, something that could happen to any one of us at any time. We feel for him more than we do an emotionless Jason Vorhees or Michael Myers[†].

In this book I'm going to look at the film itself in a minute-by-minute breakdown. I'll be looking at each character and each infamous gore effect. I'll be discussing what worked in the film and what didn't, what I feel should have and could have been done and what I feel was done perfectly. I'll be sharing reactions from critics and fans, and we'll see it's many re-titlings on video in super-collector Marc Leppla's incredible photo section. Most special of all, actress Kathleen Ferguson, who plays the doomed Barbara, sat down with me to give her first ever interview regarding NIGHTMARE, which will surely delight any fan of the film. Likewise, producer/actor Bill Milling shares some things that have *never* been revealed publicly.

Just as George Tatum *needed* to kill to express his inner, darkest feelings, this maniacal fan needed to get these thoughts out of his system ... although at this point in my life I doubt this fascination will ever be sated.

One issue that has become tiring to fans regards special effects artist Tom Savini and his involvement with the film. There is a wealth of information about this slight scandal (if you will) online. I heard Savini talk about it in person at a 1985 *Fangoria* convention in NYC[‡]. If anyone is wondering why I'm not dealing with it here is because this book is *mainly* aimed at those who love this film. We long-time fans of NIGHTMARE have read it all and there's nothing new I can provide here. To me, at this point, it's an issue I wish would just go away (and that's not a slight against Savini, an FX artist I have been in awe of since I was a kid). Note, however, there are brief mentions of the Sa vini incident during my interviews with star Kathleen Ferguson and producer Bill Milling.

As George Tatum traveled from New York to Florida, let us, too, begin our journey through a mental ward of sorts...

---

* Interview with director Romano Scavolini on the 2011 Code Red DVD release of NIGHTMARE.

† Although Jason Vorhees and Michael Myers were "normal" kids, both are quickly elevated to their own supernatural status (in both their original films and the less than stellar sequels) and cause them to become less "real" than a killer like George Tatum. Hence, audiences began to laugh and cheer on their kills. This doesn't happen in NIGHTMARE.

‡ Asked by an audience member about his involvement with the film, Savini said he was called to the set to oversee things and give a few pointers. He said everyone was doing a fine job, and that was it. He said he later sued when his name was used on posters without permission and was awarded a fair sum. (More recently, in the book *Savini: The Biography* by Tom Savini and Michael Aloisi [2019 Dark Ink]), Savini finally admits in print (and with a photo that had been circulating online for some time) that he was indeed on the set of NIGHTMARE). To add to the endless confusion, an interview extra on the 2023 Severin Blu-ray features Savini now saying he never sued or received any money.

ONE

TIMELINE FILM BREAKDOWN

with commentary

PART ONE
[00:00–03:03]*

NIGHTMARE fades in and pans across a bedroom. We see a man sweating, struggling in his sleep. This is George Tatum (played by Baird Stafford in one of only two film appearances). He wakes, tears his blanket off, and finds his bed littered with body parts. A woman's decapitated head opens its eyes to look at him, and the scene switches to George waking up screaming in a straitjacket at a mental hospital. Two orderlies enter the room and sedate him via injection *and* a handful of pills. George calms and the opening credits roll.

* Timecodes are not part of the film but for reference.

Jack Eric Williams' score kicks in as soon as the film begins. It's an extended keyboard note that instantly gives the viewer a sense of unease. The music remains at this low but eerie level even as George wakes and starts panicking at what he sees at the foot of his bed. It's not until the decapitated woman's head opens her eyes that the music hits us with a loud burst of a strong orchestra-like blast. During George's wake up and sedation, the music remains manic but slows down as the drugs quickly take effect, and as George completely calms down, the music returns to the first keyboard note heard two minutes earlier.

During the opening credits (which are simply red titles over a black background), Williams keeps the score spooky yet slightly positive. As the credits roll, the music is unsure of itself. Will the film get more intense and disturbing, or will George--who is apparently a patient at some kind of hospital--be cured of whatever's ailing?

Unlike most slasher films, NIGHTMARE doesn't open with a "20 years ago" premise, although we later learn George is haunted by an incredible act of violence he committed as a child. The film doesn't open with a masked or disguised killer taking his first victim, nor do we see a point of view shot of someone being stalked and/or killed by an unseen assailant. We're immediately confronted with a man who is evidently suffering some kind of breakdown or delusion, and we don't know right away if he is a victim, perpetrator, or both. We're not sure if NIGHTMARE will head down a supernatural path, in the same way we see premonitory dreams in other films, but the audience is interested to know why George has woken from such a disturbing dream.

The film never mentions if the hospital where George is a patient is in New York City, but the first scene of him after being released is in Times Square, so we can assume the opening sequence took place somewhere in Manhattan or close by it.

PART TWO
THE FIRST NIGHT: FLORIDA
[3:03–7:01]

We see a young woman lying on a living room floor watching TV. Children call for her to come upstairs ("Kathy come here! We need you!"). Annoyed, Kathy (Danny Ronan in her only film appearance) goes upstairs to see what the problem is. Two girls (sisters Tammy and Kim Temper, played by Tammy and Kim Peterson) claim they saw someone looking in their window, despite the fact their room is on the second floor. Kathy begs them to go to sleep and assures them no one was there. She heads back downstairs (Williams' score here is quite creepy) and we see her from outside the house, as if we're the eyes of a stalker.

Kathy tries to watch TV again but, apparently spooked by the girls' story, can't get comfortable. Dressed in a partially see-through nightgown, Kathy walks through the house looking out the windows, a trope of slasher films that was parodied at the beginning of Wes Craven's famous horror satire SCREAM (1996).

She decides to check outside (this sequence usually causes groans from the audience) and as she walks around the yard, we're the eyes of someone watching down on her from the sub-roof. We then see the rear of a dark silhouette watching her, before the camera switches to Kathy's face in the foreground, reframing the figure on the roof. A quick flashback as the figure appears to jump down on her, and then George Tatum wakes up screaming from another nightmare. We only see George for a few seconds before the film returns to the house where Kathy is babysitting. A cop car pulls in front.

A policeman checks the roof with his flashlight as an older cop watches from the side of his squad car. The senior cop phones in that they are unable to find anything amiss.

Inside the house, Kathy is sitting at the bottom of the staircase crying while being comforted by Susan Temper (Sharon Smith, who only has three other acting credits, including Herschell Gordon Lewis' 1967 musical comedy BLAST OFF GIRLS!). Susan tells Kathy to relax, that it was probably just someone playing a trick.

We see Susan's third child, C.J. (played by C.J. Cooke in his only screen appearance), sitting at the top of the stairs with a shit-eating grin before covering his mouth so his mother doesn't hear him laugh. C.J. is a practical joker, and the soundtrack gets a bit silly to enhance this fact.

Although the implication is that C.J. jumped on her from the roof (the sequence is very fast and unclear), it makes more sense that Kathy had seen the dark figure on the roof and called the police. Had C.J. actually jumped on her, she would've easily recognized him (he uses the same disguise to scare her in a later bathroom scene). Kathy doesn't complain to Susan about C.J. as she does his coming pranks.

(You may have noticed: the actors playing the three Temper children use their real names. Perhaps one of the filmmakers figured this would be easier for them? And while I remember, late night TV commercials for NIGHTMARE featured a tag line saying something to the effect of "And introducing C.J. Cooke," I can't find this on any DVD or Blu-ray extras, nor has it surfaced on YouTube.)

PART THREE
THE FIRST NIGHT: NEW YORK
[7:00–17:06]

George Tatum is sleeping restlessly. Flashes of a nightmare about a man being tied up; flashback to George twitching in bed, with a tense soundtrack. We see a young boy watching a man being smacked by a woman, then the boy fleeing down a staircase. Blood is spattered around the room but we don't know what's causing it. We see a gruesome clip of a decapitated body as George wakes up screaming, sitting in a well-lit room in a straitjacket.

The scene changes to someone looking at documents, apparently in another room at the institution. George's face is seen on four TV monitors along with statistics on a fifth screen. When the man at the table gets up (with a large cigar in his mouth), the camera zooms in on the middle TV monitor, which reads:

PATIENT: TATUM
CASE # 5306-8A
DIAGNOSIS:
SCHIZOPHRENIA
MILD AMNESIA
HOMICIDAL DREAM FIXATION
SEIZURES

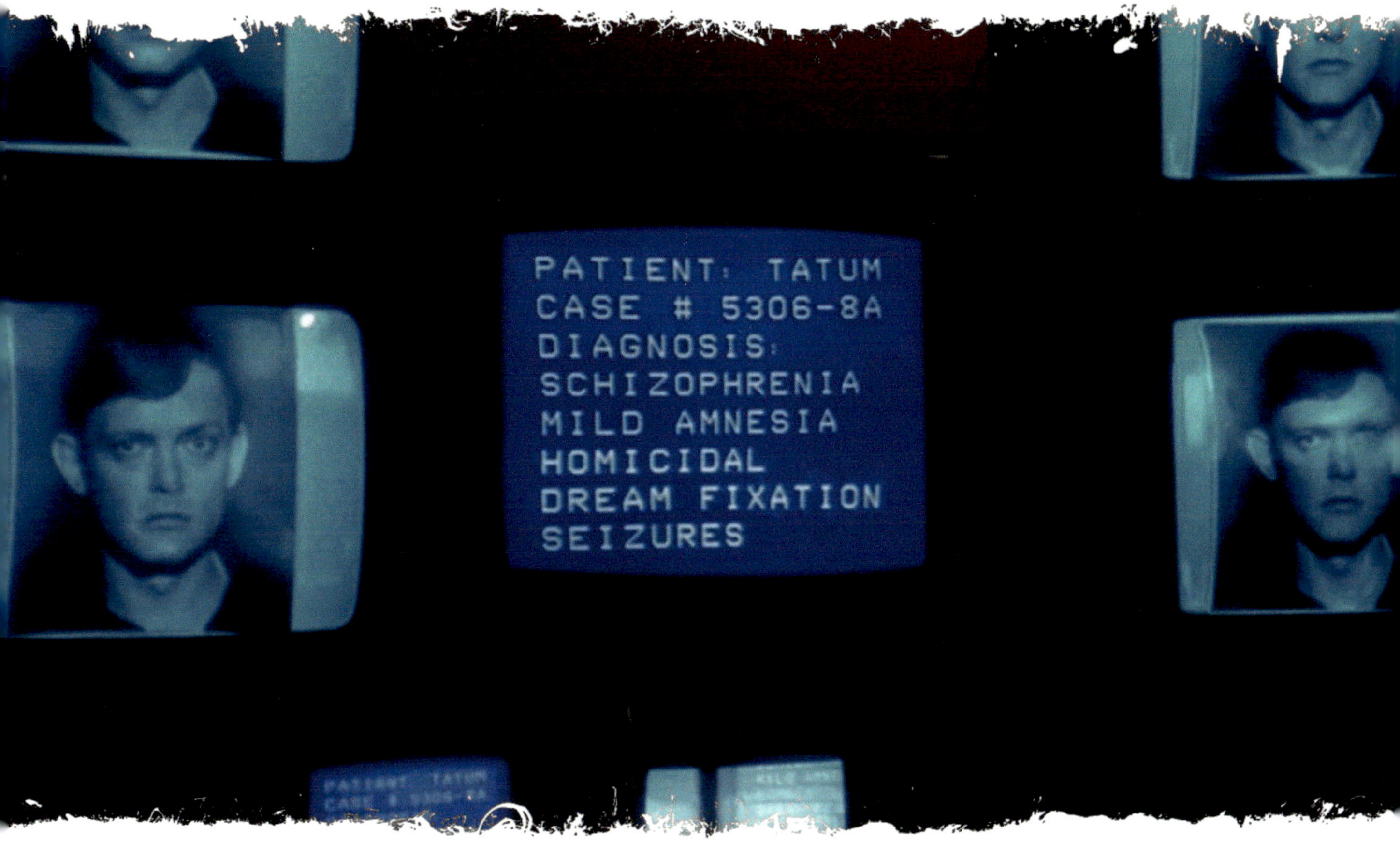

George Tatum is then seen walking into a small conference room, neatly dressed in a white dress shirt and black vest. Doctors, including the cigar smoking man, are observing through a two-way mirror.

George lights a cigarette and looks at the mirror as if he can see behind it, causing one of the technicians to shut the lights off.

George's doctor, Dr. Williams (played by Bill Milling, one of four producers of the film), enters the room. We hear the man with the cigar, John Watkins, explaining to the people behind the double mirror that Tatum has been Williams' patient for over a year. He explains that experimental drugs have helped to ease George's "violent episodes", yet haven't stopped the dreams, which Tatum refuses to talk about.

Watkins orders someone to turn the sound on in the conference room and we hear Dr. Williams and Tatum speaking.

George talks about his recurring nightmare. Sometimes he feels that he's the child, and at other times it's like the child is just standing there … then he has a light outburst claiming the child can't be him and that "it's not a weapon."

This mysterious interview gives NIGHTMARE a heavy chill factor. It's obvious to the audience that this is a partial look at George's childhood killing, yet George is fighting to remember it, perhaps due to the drugs he's been given.

He then tells Dr. Williams that whenever the dream reveals a hatchet, that's when he's woken up and given pills by the institution's staff. Then the dream and the memories vanish.

Williams pats George on the arm and says he thinks they've just had a good session. I recall the audience laughing at this statement the first time I saw the film; Bill Milling isn't exactly the best actor there is, although personally I think he does a good enough job.

We're back in the monitor room as Watkins (another of the film's four producers) records on audiocassette Tatum's history. We learn that he has come from Braston State Hospital for the Criminally Insane after being arrested as a suspect in a sexual assault on a Brooklyn family. He then explains George's schizophrenic tendencies and the medication he believes has helped him. Watkins states Tatum's schizophrenic tendencies have been extinguished and his other issues either modified or controlled. Prognosis? George Tatum is their first major success and Watkins believes they have taken a "dangerous psychotic and completely rebuilt him."

He then adds, "Programming him for future government or private sector use will be our next step." This comment brings an almost conspiratorial angle to the film that's never developed.

Watkins congratulates everyone involved in Tatum's rehabilitation.

The scene flashes to George Tatum in Times Square, walking past sleazy movie theaters and sex shops. We assume he has been released although this isn't confirmed until later.

Times Square fans will be in their element during these shots, which show some great theater marquees, including an all-out CALIGULA display, one for the Gene Wilder/ Richard Pryor film STIR CRAZY, and several porno theaters. George finally steps into one of the latter, Show World.

George pays his admission and goes downstairs to a peep show and into a small booth that allows him to look out on a topless woman. About to feel her breasts, he suddenly has a flashback to his violent nightmare, then his time runs out and the booth window closes, cutting him off from the rest of the strip tease. He leaves distraught and walks around before being lured into a "one on one" booth. Here a girl named Tara speaks to him in his booth via a telephone, starts using a vibrator, and asks whether George would like to do this to her. He starts having flashbacks to his gory nightmare, revealing more of that scene to us.

Unable to accept the dream — or Tara, who is getting more explicit — George collapses to the floor, foaming at the mouth like a rabid dog. The booth window closes.

Back at the institution, Watkins is reading the digital print-out of his recorded notes, toking on his unlit cigar. We see a computer screen scroll, "inform the military," suggesting there may be more to the experimental drugs than meets the eye.

The sequence where George visits Show World gives NIGHTMARE much of its sleaze factor. As a rite of passage for many NY teenage boys at the time, I too visited the notorious sex emporium with my buddies during our high school years in the mid-1980s. It was every bit as nasty as the scenes depicted in the movie — perhaps worse! While many "regular" films (notably TAXI DRIVER [1976]) feature shots of Times Square during its infamous "sleaze era," few convey the sense of grittiness as

NIGHTMARE does. To have it documented forever is either a blessing or a curse.

THE SECOND DAY
[17:07–27:11]

George Tatum is on the Staten Island Ferry, leaving Manhattan.

If you've never seen NIGHTMARE, and are from this area, do your best not to get irritated. I think Scavolini did a well enough job getting Tatum out of the city, even if going through Staten Island isn't the easiest way to do so. Nevertheless, as a native Islander, I'm always thrilled when the Ferry shows up in films (as it also does in Lucio Fulci's THE NEW YORK RIPPER [1982]).

Of course, in our post 9/11 world, the shot of the World Trade Center fading into the distance as the boat floats away from Manhattan conjures a sense of loss no one would have predicted back when the film was first released. That might be said of any film featuring the towers, but in one with such a dark tone it evokes an even deeper sense of dread.

Back at the institution, Dr. Williams is checking his watch and asking his secretary if Tatum has arrived for his appointment. Frustrated, he continues to wait as we see Tatum make his way through the Staten Island side of the ferry terminal.

Tatum walks up to a phone booth and makes a call.

The phone rings in the Florida home of the Temper family. Young C.J. answers but hangs up when no one speaks. His mom asks who was on the phone, then tells C.J. to hurry up before he misses his school bus.

Back on Staten Island, George stares across NY harbor, looking at Manhattan, possibly contemplating if he should go to his appointment with Dr. Williams. He discards a cigarette and gets into a car. Is the vehicle stolen or has he managed to rent one very quickly? This is another of NIGHTMARE's many continuity problems.

Back in Florida, Susan Temper wakes to start her day and furnishes the film with one of its few nude scenes. She gets out of bed, throws on a bathrobe, and heads to the bathroom. I'm surprised she wasn't in more films as she is a capable actor with the aura of a leading lady.

George is seen speeding down an open highway, listening to a Philadelphia radio station. Philly is a good two hours from Staten Island, depending on traffic, and the soundtrack here is a haunting, mellow tune.

Susan is out of the shower and getting ready for her day, beginning with a trip on her boyfriend Bob's yacht. Bob is played by Mik Cribben, another production manager, still photographer and sound editor on the film, with an impressive list of horror and exploitation films to his credit, plus big budget sound department work on the likes of SPIDER-MAN (2002) and Penn and Teller's TV series BULLSHIT! He's a tall guy and his character in NIGHTMARE — bearded and seemingly carefree — hints at a hippy past.

Tatum drives through a toll plaza in North Carolina, and if you haven't figured it out by now, he's apparently heading to Florida to "visit" the Tempers.

Susan and Bob sail off the Florida coast as Bob sings silly pirate songs. He says, while steering the ship, "You know, sometimes I think in another life I used to be a pirate." Critics may scoff at such dialogue, but I find it fun, and the three different audiences with which I've experienced the film theatrically all laughed at his goofy comment.

What I don't find fun is Susan, sitting on the deck on a beautiful Sunny day in a black turtleneck sweater! This has baffled me more over the years than the film's plot inconsistencies.

On the highway again, the radio in George's car informs us he's entering Myrtle Beach, South Carolina (damn is this guy driving fast!). The DJ announces a popular cover band playing at a beach-side bar. George runs into some car trouble, and we see him next on the side of the road with the hood popped open. He fiddles around but it's apparent he knows little to nothing about car engines. Pissed, he punches the hood and kicks the passenger side door closed.

At a nightclub called Gatsby's, George is sitting at the bar listening to a cowboy-looking singer with an acoustic guitar. He goes outside for a smoke (I like to think it's because he hates country music as much as I do) where he watches a woman get in her car after kissing her boyfriend goodnight. The poor bastard tries to go home with her, but she asks him to please understand, "not tonight, okay?" He acquiesces and says he'll call her later.

As she takes off down a dark road, tense music comes in. I think NIGHTMARE's soundtrack is criminally underrated, and this sequence is evidence of the fact. A shot from the backseat suggests George may be hiding, but we can't be certain, even as she pulls into her driveway.

Inside the house, she undresses and gets ready for a shower.

Her boyfriend Steve calls from the bar, and we see her leave the bathroom in a towel to answer the phone. While checking why there is static on the line, George pops up behind her with a demented grin.

The tired horror film trope — a person bending down to reveal a killer behind them — has been done countless times, but Scavolini makes it work with the combination of Stafford's perfectly evil facial expression and a quickly manic jump in the soundtrack.

Evidently, he was hiding in the backseat the whole time. Steve should definitely get his eyesight checked.

As Steve pointlessly clicks his pay phone trying to get a connection (has this ever really worked?), George grabs the woman by the chin from behind and slices her across the throat with a knife. We see a close-up of the neck opening and blood running down her neck. George's facial expression when the knife finishes its work is terrifying, almost as if he is *sexually satisfied*. Letting the body fall to the carpet, we're hit with arguably the most disgusting gurgling sounds ever committed to a scene of this nature.

George slowly sits down on her stomach as his nightmare flashbacks come back to haunt him. He stabs her slowly in the stomach four times, his face again adopting the look of sex. He then leans down and whispers "I'm sorry" to his victim. Distraught and in intense mental anguish, sweat drops from George's forehead onto the corpse, then we get another glimpse of his nightmare: a young boy closes a door.

George licks the blood off his hands, and his nightmare flashback ends with thoughts of the decapitated head we saw at the beginning of the film.

There have been some realistic throat slashing sequences in cinema. There are many more realistic than the one just described, but few pack such a punch on both a gross out *and* emotional level. I for one nearly gagged the first time I saw it play out on the big screen and suspect even the most jaded gorehound will be quieted by it. We care for this victim we know next to nothing about.

George's first post-institution victim is named Barbara, played by Kathleen Ferguson who appeared in only three films, one being another slasher outing from 1984 titled SILENT MADNESS (released theatrically in 3D, yet as forgettable as they come). Her role here is small but, to this film geek at least, unforgettable.

THE THIRD DAY
[27:12–48:19]

The morning after George's brutal throat slashing, we see him lying on his stomach in a hotel room, contemplating the ghastly deed. This quick sequence ends, as did the first kill, with a flash of the decapitated head from George's nightmare.

Back in Manhattan, Watkins is saying how no one knows where George is, not even Dr. Williams, who is standing across the room listening to Watkins' reprimand. One of the most unintentionally funny scenes in slasher film history follows.

Dr. Williams says, "For what it's worth, I'm sorry."

With overacting worthy of an Academy Award, Watkins replies: "Sorry?! You lose a dangerously psychotic patient from a secret experimental drug program and all you can say is I'm Sorry?!" Trust me, you *have* to see this with an audience to fully appreciate it.

Watkins asks Williams if he checked George's job, only to find he left two weeks ago. Apparently, Tatum had been working somewhere and living in some kind of home that was separate from the institution, which in itself is hard to buy. Williams is still convinced Tatum "is not dangerous," to which Watkins replies, "You're a bigger schmuck than I thought you were."

I don't often care for moments of humor in horror films, but this, which I'm quite sure was unintentional, works. Watkins' high-pitched voice, coupled with the extra long stogie sticking out of his mouth, always invites laughter.

Watkins warns Williams to get Tatum back to the hospital before things "get out of hand," not knowing things already have, many miles away.

In a moment of intentional humor, as soon as Watkins tells Williams to "Get off your ass and find him," we're treated to a close-up of George's ass (in a pair of white briefs) getting out of a motel bed. Simple, but to me, pure genius.

George washes up in front of the bathroom mirror, takes a handful of pills, and we see flashes of the boy from his nightmare, this time covered in blood. George remains disturbed by his actions the night before.

Next, we're in Susan Temper's bedroom as she talks on the phone with Bob. He begs her to come and see him again, and she eventually agrees.

During this conversation, a flute-sounding piece of music (that's used in various scenes) adds a haunting ambiance. The use of this song, especially during the grim finale, burrows into the viewer's head.

The song carries into the next scene, comprising George on the road again in a new car, heading toward Florida. We become aware via the voice of a radio DJ that George has reached Daytona Beach, home to the Tempers.

It's hard to be hit by it on a single viewing, but after watching NIGHTMARE as many times as I have, this flash from Susan on the phone to George in his car creates a palpable tension. NIGHTMARE isn't an action-packed film, but the growing sense of dread is pulled off well, which, again, I believe in large part can be credited to the score.

The three Temper kids come home from school. After yelling for their mother to open the door, the girls help boost C.J. onto the sub-roof which he climbs to enter through a window.

Meanwhile, their mother Susan is on Bob's yacht again, making out on a lower deck bed, topless, like a horny teenager. She realizes she's too late to be home before her kids.

C.J. enters the house through a bedroom window then runs downstairs to let his sisters in, whereupon the older sister reminds him to take the garbage out. Talk about a sibling being ungrateful!

On the yacht, Susan is trying to pry Bob off her. He thinks of anything to get her to stay ("Come on … one afternoon they can make their own peanut butter sandwiches."). Besides the aforementioned dialogue from John Watkins, this comment from Bob is the only other time NIGHTMARE usually gets laughs from an audience, at least on the three occasions I've seen it on the big screen.

C.J. takes the trash out to the curb and the soundtrack warns us something isn't right. Across the street, a man in a trenchcoat steps out from behind a tree. It's George Tatum. C.J. evidently doesn't recognize him, but George is reminded of the child from his recurring nightmare.

Back on the love boat, Susan goes on deck as Bob yells, "Woman, you are torturing me! I have needs! I'm a human being!" She calls home to check on the kids as Bob finally pulls his pants on.

The phone rings as C.J. comes back into the house, painfully holding his stomach. Blood is all over his white shirt. His two sisters scream. Kim answers the phone and tells her mother that C.J. is hurt. Susan panics and Bob tells her he'll drive her home.

It should be pointed out that the acting of real life sisters Tammy and Kim in this particular sequence is terrible. They query the bloody C.J. with all the concern of someone on a month-paid vacation.

Bob tries to keep Susan calm as they speed toward the house. The film splits its time between quick cuts of Bob and Susan driving and C.J. pushing his sister away from his bloody stomach. We assume that George must've stabbed him. C.J.'s acting isn't quite believable either, but considering what's about to happen, I'm still on the fence as to whether it's good or not.

Susan and Bob run into the house. Bob kneels and assures C.J. everything is going to be alright. When Bob asks how he got like this, C.J. groans that a man out by the street tried to kill him with a knife.

Susan kneels behind Bob, who manages to get C.J.'s hands off his stomach. He lifts C.J.'s shirt, swipes his belly, then tastes the blood.

"It's ketchup," he says all-to-calmly, and C.J. starts to giggle.

Susan has a minor freak out. She says she knew he was pulling a prank by the look in his eyes and that she has had it with him. She sends him upstairs to bed.

Bob assures Susan that his son is just "a little too imaginative", that "he's not a gangster." I love this guy!

Susan takes her anger out on her two innocent daughters, telling the older one she should've known better.

"I hate this fucking house. You know I've hated this house since the day he left?" First time viewers usually miss this line, or don't get it, but it's a reference to her husband (or ex-husband, we're never told). Apparently, her husband left the day after C.J.'s birth.

Bob proves that he's not just after a piece of ass, telling Susan that he cares about her and the kids. She can see he means it. He has a sip of Scotch with Susan, then tells the kids he's taking them out to McDuff's to get a fish dinner. I'm not from Florida so I'm not sure if McDuff's was a real place. It sounds legit.

Susan, Bob, and the two girls hop in Bob's car and take off without telling C.J. I'd like to think Susan isn't that much of a bitch. Then again…

As soon as they leave, the phone rings and C.J. goes downstairs to answer.

In his motel room, George hangs up as soon as he hears C.J.'s voice, and it's at this point we suspect that somehow he knows the Temper family.

Spooked, C.J. looks around the empty house. He carefully makes his way back up to his bedroom. This sequence is quite creepy, between the soundtrack and knowing that C.J. had recently seen a strange man right across the street from the house. It's a fear everyone experiences at some point in their childhood, and here Scavolini captures it perfectly.

Back in Manhattan, John Watkins, wearing a trenchcoat over his shoulders like he's some kind of Count, enters his office in the middle of the night to look at one of George Tatum's files. I'm still not sure if he's trying to see how long he has been missing, or fathom some other unexplained statistic, but either way Watkins shakes his head and leaves the office. It's a weird sequence and one that, to me, is a minute of pointless filler. However, I do get a kick out of Watkins, even when he's not saying anything with his silly sounding voice, so we'll let it slide.

C.J. is woken by a friend outside his window. C.J. tells him he can't come down because he's being punished. The friend informs him he "Has his stuff," and throws a small bag up to the second floor, which of course C.J. catches on the first try. His friend takes off.

Downstairs, Kathy the babysitter is trying to help Kim with her homework, but Kim is being silly. Tired of the girls' wisecracks, she tells them both to get ready for bed because it's past 10 o'clock. This makes me wonder about C.J.'s friend: do his parents know he's out running around so late?

As the girls get ready for bed, C.J. is in his unlit room working on what is undoubtedly his next prank. One sister knocks on his door to see if he is okay but, busy with a pair of electrical pliers and wire, he doesn't answer.

Kathy tells the girls to be quiet, then she shuts all the lights on the first floor off. The phone rings. No one answers. It rings again as soon as Kathy hangs up, but again no one answers her. She sits on the bottom step, spooked, when the phone rings a third time. This time she looks upstairs, as if suddenly aware that C.J. is up to his usual mischief.

She busts his door open hoping to catch him, but he has already jumped beneath the bed covers. Kathy is convinced he was asleep, although the audience can't be sure whether it was C.J. or George who made the calls.

Hang-up-phone-calls are another trope, but again, in NIGHTMARE, it works. This sequence is even creepier than the earlier scene where C.J. carefully jogs back to his room. We know Kathy is frightened and annoyed, this sense captured perfectly in the musical accompaniment.

When Kathy shuts the door, C.J. sticks his tongue out at her and blows a raspberry. It's funny, something that many viewers can recall doing in their own childhood.

Kathy goes back downstairs and listens in on the phone which she had left off the hook. The sequence continues its creepy tone despite C.J.'s silly outburst.

One thing about the Temper house: there are a *lot* of windows. The kitchen Kathy walks around is more window than wall, and the small hallway where the phone is mounted is next to the front door, which is also mostly window. The first time I saw the film I was expecting George to crash through one of the many windows at any second. Despite having seen the film countless times, I still get the willies during this segment.

The sequence ends with Kathy standing across the hall from the phone, waiting for another call. But the film moves on.

George drives down to the beach and removes his throat-slashed victim from the trunk. She is wrapped in a black garbage bag, but with her neck and head sticking out. George lays her on the sand, looks at her, then brings her to him in a hug. We can feel his sorrow. We know he can't control what he does. After a moment of silence, George lifts his head to the sky and lets out an agonizing shriek. He lays the body back down, rests his head on her chest, and cries, much as he had done when he murdered her.

With only one scream, Baird Stafford conveys the angst felt by George Tatum. I didn't think much of the scene the first few times I watched it, but today I consider it an incredible piece of acting. It's the first time in the film we truly sympathize with Tatum, knowing he is totally schizophrenic.

Kathy tidies up the house and decides to take a shower while at the same time we see a dark figure walk by the front door. The camera cuts between Kathy and the anonymous figure as it makes its way through the house, finding the stairs that lead to the second floor.

We know the three children are sleeping.

Kathy wraps a towel around her hair and stands before the bathroom sink, where she slides the medicine cabinet open to get toothpaste. When she closes the mirrored cabinet door, we see the reflection of a man standing in the hallway with glowing red eyes.

Kathy screams, turns around and pushes the man, who falls back into the wall.

It turns out C.J. has perfected the dummy seen earlier in the film: his face is sticking out of the dummy's chest, while the Halloween mask with flashing eyes sits above him on a rigged contraption.

C.J. says, a spoiled immature brat, "Nanny nanny boo boo! Stick your head in doo doo!" Then he blows another raspberry at his babysitter.

The sequence ends. If it wasn't clear before, C.J. Temper is not only a *serious* practical joker, but also a real prick! You half admire his dedication to scaring the crap out of people. Despite his mother's punishment, he still managed to acquire material from his friend, construct a glowing-eyed dummy that stands about six feet tall, and scare the shit out of his babysitter for the umpteenth time (in the next sequence, Kathy explains that she can't take his pranks anymore). C.J. may be one of the most annoying and, I hate to admit, one of the *coolest* kids in slasher film history.

However, C.J. Cooke's acting chops are still questionable at this point in the film. The earlier scene, in which he feigns his own stabbing, saw him smirk in ways that could be construed as either poor acting, or genius. The same here. When he is unmasked as the mastermind behind the six-foot dummy, his bratty school-yard mock song sounds kind of stupid, but perhaps that's the brilliance of it?

THE FOURTH DAY
[48:20–58:00]

This segment begins with Kathy telling Susan she can no longer babysit for C.J. She swears he's evil and Susan doesn't disagree with her! Kathy walks away from the house and sees C.J. looking at her from his second-floor bedroom window.

Flash to a real estate office, where Susan has decided to put the house up for sale. The real estate agent is played by Ray Baker, another actor in his only film appearance. He asks Susan to have some pictures of the house taken and they set up a time for him to view the property. He believes the house will sell quickly.

Then we're in front of the house as Bob snaps pictures. "Asking me to take a Polaroid is like asking Picasso to paint your car," he says to Susan, insinuating the task is beneath him.

Following this humorous interaction, the film dives into what is perhaps its eeriest moment. Bob gives one of his Polaroids a double-take, and asks, "There's nobody in the house, is there?" A single note on the soundtrack creates instant tension.

They both notice a man's figure in a picture of a second-floor window, but looking up at the window, they see no one there, and run in the house to investigate.

Susan asks, "Who's in there?" before following Bob upstairs. The POV is that of Bob as he looks in each room on the second floor. Bob is convinced no one is present and that both their imaginations are being "Affected by C.J.'s."

The couple stand in the hallway discussing how the figure could have been a shadow or illusion, but the view we have of them is from within a closet.

With a loud single note on the soundtrack, a man's foot slides back into the closet. Sure enough, George Tatum is spying on the couple. He holds a knife at the ready but doesn't use it. He hears Bob say that they should pick the kids up after school and go to the beach.

This sequence gets the goosebumps going quite well, playing on a familiar fear of someone lurking inside our home.

Back in Manhattan at the institute, Watkins tries to figure out where George has gone. The computer tells him Tatum's car has been found in Myrtle Beach, South Carolina. Watkins ponders this development as he chews on his never-ending cigar. He learns that another car from South Carolina is missing and the owner

is presumed dead. A co-worker next to Watkins whistles at the news of the car owner's apartment being discovered filled with blood.

After some more frantic typing, the computer divulges that Tatum's most likely destination is Daytona Beach, Florida. Watkins tells his partner they'd better go find him.

In Florida we're on the beach with Bob, Susan, and the three Temper kids, with Susan yelling at C.J. for feeding and attracting birds. C.J. runs off with his binoculars, looking down the beach, where he spies the same trenchcoated man seen earlier outside the house. The man looks back at C.J., prompted him to run back to his mother, saying a man is following him. Susan yells at him again, sick of his joking around, as Bob tells her to relax and takes C.J. for a walk.

C.J. swears to Bob he isn't lying about the man, yet Bob reminds him that his stories and pranks are giving him a bad reputation. He tells C.J. that he's "sort of" the man of the house and that he needs to take care of his mother.

Looking through C.J.'s binoculars, Bob sees the guy in the trenchcoat and asks whether it's the same man C.J. has been talking about, C.J. isn't sure and sounds genuinely disappointed that no one believes him.

The two share a tender moment. C.J. asks whether Bob is going to marry his mother. The sequence ends with Susan staring off into the ocean, and George standing down the beach.

You can't help but like Bob at this point. Up to now, he seemed only interested in getting into Susan's pants, but here we learn he's not simply crazy about her but very proud to think that one day he'll be C.J.'s father. Any man who doesn't mind being with a woman with three kids is a stand-up guy.

A phone call in the middle of the night wakes Susan from her bed. On the line, a man's voice tells her that he wants her, that he has seen her legs, and that she is sleeping in *his* bed. She threatens to call the police, but the man goes on to say he knows she's alone. "I'm coming…" the voice says when she slams the receiver down and lights a cigarette,

The scene ends with Susan rubbing her forehead, wondering what is going on in her hopefully soon-to-be-sold house.

Phone call scenes like this are a staple of slasher films, and I think this one scores 100% on the creep factor. Actor Baird Stafford said he hated the sequence* as he felt the threatening phone call was out of character. Maybe so, but I still think it's effective.

THE FIFTH DAY

[58:01–1:07:59]

In Manhattan, Dr. Milling receives a phone call from George. George is crying, trying to tell him how his problem is stronger than the pills. Milling assures him that he's his friend and tries to discover his whereabouts.

When Milling says, "It's only a dream, and dreams can't hurt you," George once again has a flashback to the violent murder that has been haunting him. He falls off the bed in his motel room and begins foaming at the mouth. I assumed this is a reaction to his meds, but either way it's quite disgusting.

The scene cuts to C.J. riding his bicycle down a seaside road. He passes a teenage girl jogging, who says hello to him (her name is Candy, played by Candy Marchese in her only credited film role). He runs into his friend Tony, also on a bike, who says he needs to stop home. C.J. asks him to bring "the other guys" back with him.

Candy spots C.J.'s bike parked outside of an abandoned house near the shore. She goes in calling and looking for him. Classic slasher film mistake! Upstairs, still calling his name, and despite seeing rats scurrying around, she continues her search.

Slowly, the camera reveals George Tatum standing behind her. The camera cuts to a broken doll laying on an old mattress and we hear her murder. Why Scavolini decided to feature this kill scene off-screen is anyone's guess, but I'll lay odds it was the inability to get an FX crew in on the day of the shoot.

C.J.'s friend Tony then comes to the same abandoned house, notices C.J.'s bike, and goes inside calling for him. We see C.J. playing alongside the house when he hears his friend calling, but he decides not to answer and initially remains outside with a grin on his face.

He then calls to Tony, now exploring the second floor. Tony says that C.J. should come on up and see "all this neat stuff." C.J. claims he has to leave and takes off on his bike just as Tony notices an old mirror. The mirror tips

* Baird states this in an interview extra on the Code Red DVD.

over and he finds the corpse of Candy, bloodied up with a rat on her shoulder. He calls out to C.J., and we see George Tatum's shadow coming up the stairs.

Tony screams.

I always found this sequence tedious and unnecessary. Just why is George Tatum hiding out in an abandoned house when he has a nice comfy motel to wait in until nightfall? That Candy and Tony go inside the house looking for C.J. is improbable, too. The scene is set up to make C.J. a suspect in the murders, but I think it could've been done another way. And considering NIGHTMARE revels in its gore FX, I'm still surprised we don't see Candy's death as graphically as the others, although it is understandable they kept young Tony's death off screen. That C.J. takes off after Tony shows up is odd, too, as he had been waiting for him to return with their other friends.

It should also be noted that Candy Marchese and Geoffrey Marchese (who plays Tony) are either real life siblings or mother and son.

That night at the Temper house, Susan is trying to talk on the phone and serve her kids dinner as they argue at the table. As she yells at them to be quiet, the kids notice cars pull up out front and yell, "Mom! Cops!"

Susan runs outside to see what's happening, and turns around to look accusingly at C.J. through the window. One of his sisters says, "He's gonna get it now."

C.J. is driven to the abandoned house by his mother and they're met by the police as bodies are being taken out on stretchers, covered in sheets.

An official of some sort removes the sheet from Tony's face, and asks C.J., "You know him, don't you?" He then asks C.J. his age (nine) and whether he knows what happened to Tony. C.J. shakes his head, assures him he didn't see anything, and the man claims his friends knew he was there.

C.J. is asked whether he hurt his friend, to which he quietly replies, "I didn't kill him."

In an unintentionally funny scene, Susan seems to comfort her disturbed son, pushing the hair out of his face, then, when the cops dismiss them, she puts C.J. back in her car and tells him to "Shut up!" when he asks, "Mommy, what happened?"

Ultimately, this is one of several segments in which the involvement of children adds to the film's overall dark tone. With C.J. now a suspect, we wonder if Susan is starting to believe her little boy is more than a prankster.

THE FINAL DAY
[1:08:02–1:30:28]

We now enter NIGHTMARE's finale, which lasts over a half hour.

Two policemen, at dawn, locate another car abandoned by George.

The Manhattan institute's computer shows us that police have forwarded the info. See? Internet-like technology has been around a lot longer than you may think!

In the Temper house, we're the eyes of George as he again has gained entrance and is scouting out the second floor. He takes a pair of pink panties from Susan's bureau and holds them to his face and sweats onto them. He then looks up to the ceiling as if asking for divine guidance.

C.J. comes home from school, calling out

loud to his mom. Without waiting for a response, he says that his teacher sent him home because all the other kids think he killed Tony.

George returns the panties as C.J. goes upstairs still calling for his mom. George manages to sneak into a closet and tries to open his bottle of pills. As C.J. goes from room to room, George gets the bottle open, but a few pills fly out into the hallway. C.J. notices them (but not George's shoes, visible through the open closet door!) and takes them downstairs, sets them up on the dining room table, and starts to examine them when the phone rings.

Upstairs George is on the line saying, "Leave this house … while you can."

I always wondered how this worked. A few slasher films feature phone calls being made from within the same house. Did people tend to have separate landlines in their homes back then? I guess so. Before the age of cell phones, how else could scenes like this be pulled off? Yet another scene we'll just let slide…

C.J. thinks it's his friend Peter, but the man's voice again warns him to get out of the house. C.J. hangs up and continues examining the pills.

The film then cuts to a shot of a plane landing, keeping us in suspense of the goings on at the Temper house.

Dr. Williamson has arrived and meets Watkins' co-worker at the airport. They rush to a car where Watkins is waiting, toking on his ever-present unlit cigar.

On the ride to Daytona, Williamson swears George isn't there, because he "knows his patient." Watkins goes on to say that newspaper articles he has researched place someone with George's same last name in Daytona years ago, when a couple was murdered with an axe. This corresponds with the nightmares that have been plaguing George.

As Williamson gets upset, Watkins assures him that although he was rehabilitated with their experimental drugs, George is now "Out there killing people … and we can't have that."

This line of dialogue always gets laughs from the audience, and rightfully so. The statement is just so silly it's amazing it made it to the final version of the script.

At the Temper house, Susan is getting dressed to go to a business party for Bob. She's begging Kathy to please come over and babysit the kids one more time. She assures Kathy C.J. has promised not to cause any more trouble, and that it'll just be for two hours. Kathy eventually agrees.

Cut to a quick scene at said business party, where someone is pushed into the pool, while the rest of the guests stand around talking and drinking as if nothing has happened. Are we to assume pranks like this are commonplace at business parties? Susan chats with Bob.

At the Temper house, Kathy makes sure the kids are asleep, then heads downstairs and turns off all the lights. Although C.J. has scared her in the past, it doesn't dissuade her from sitting in front of the TV tuned to a horror movie.

A door creaks open behind her.

She doesn't notice as the sound is drowned by a woman screaming on the television. We see a pair of hands about to strangle her, but the man's face comes into view and it's not George Tatum.

Turns out Kathy's sister told her boyfriend Joey where she was at, and he snuck over to get high (and laid). Joey, played by Tommy

Bouvier in his — you guessed it! — only credited film role, is a typical slasher film idiot teenager with the voice to go with the character. He sounds high as a kite the second he starts talking, and we have to wonder if someone as good looking as Kathy couldn't find anyone better in all of Daytona.

Joe carries Kathy into the next room where they fall on the floor and roll around, kissing and undressing each other as we see the silhouette of a man pass by the back door window.

Then we're the eyes of the creeping man, who we assume is George Tatum. We don't see how he got inside the house, but after all the scares you'd think Susan or Bob would've made it a bit harder to do so.

From the kitchen, still through the prowler's eyes, we witness Joey on top of Kathy. For an R-rated scene it's a bit graphic, with Joey's ass going up and down between Kathy's legs, wrapped around his back.

As soon as they're done, Joey says he could use another smoke and crawls around the floor looking for his joint while Kathy heads upstairs to take a shower. He sits on the short staircase between floors smoking it, and we see flashes of Kathy in the shower.

While Joey is getting high, George comes up behind him wearing the bald-headed mask* C.J. had used to prank Kathy earlier. George strangles Joey with a wire of some sort as Kathy calls for him. George drags him into the next room just as she enters.

In a bathrobe with a towel on her head, Kathy calls for Joey quietly as if to not wake the kids. Then she notices the man standing atop the short staircase. She thinks it's C.J. pulling another prank and yells at him for being out of bed.

George approaches her slowly with a small pickaxe in his hand. Kathy says, "That's it, I'm calling your mother," and as she reaches for the phone, George grabs her arm and nails it to the table with the pickaxe. Kathy screams and George delivers a series of blows to her back, shown in gruesome close-up. This sequence is particularly disturbing, especially when the camera moves and we see C.J. has been woken and is watching the carnage from the staircase.

He runs upstairs as George hears him calling for his sisters to wake up.

Just as George is about to follow upstairs (C.J.'s sisters think he's playing a joke on them), the phone rings, and George decides to go answer it. When he picks up, Susan says, "Kathy, what took you so long to answer? Are the kids asleep?" George remains silent as he hangs the phone up. The angle of shot adds to the tension of the scene. George looks very creepy in the old man mask.

Upstairs, C.J. picks up the phone but his mother has already hung up. He realizes the masked man is in the hallway, so locks his mother's bedroom door and starts searching through her dresser drawers for something — a weapon? George begins hacking a hole in the door with the pickaxe, bringing the classic Jack Nicholson scene from THE SHINING (1980) to mind. These shots are filmed from the floor and give the scene an incredibly claustrophobic feel.

* It's a Don Post mask from 1979–80, sold as "The Sheik", except that in the film it's bald and without the turban it was originally sold with. I've been looking for one ever since my first viewing of the film.

On the ninth whack, George makes a head-sized hole in the door (a regular axe would've saved him some time). C.J. finds a handgun under his mother's bed and shoots George's hand as it reaches in to open the door. George screams as C.J. fires a second shot into his stomach. We see George slowly fall to the floor.

George tries to pull himself up by holding the pickaxe which is still stuck in the door, only to have C.J. put another three bullets in his belly.

The first few times I saw NIGHTMARE I laughed at this. But might George's strength and resilience have something to do with the medication and military interests Watkins mentioned earlier? We will never know.

C.J. peeks through the hole in the door and watches the masked man fall down, holding his stomach. When he is sure the man is done moving, he gets his sisters and they run downstairs. To the credit of the filmmakers, George doesn't try to grab one of them.

As the kids run outside calling for the neighbors to help, we see George twitch and use the pickaxe to try to gain purchase on the carpet. Meanwhile, C.J. attempts to phone for help from the first floor phone as his sisters remain outside yelling.

They alert C.J. to the fact that George is headed down the stairs, upon which their brother fires the final bullet at the masked man's stomach. I always count bullets in films, and it brings a smile to my face anytime a film doesn't turn a 6-chamber pistol into an endless machine gun.

The three kids run away from the house. One sister asks where Kathy is and screams when C.J. tells her she's dead.

George starts hyperventilating atop the small staircase. He sits up and yells something that causes C.J. to say "He's still alive!"

His sisters tell him he's crazy for going back in, but C.J. tells them not to worry, he still has the gun.

George is missing and oddly there's no blood on the staircase despite his stomach being a bloody mess. C.J. decides to head back upstairs and finish him off, but we assume there are no more bullets in his pistol.

As C.J. carefully makes his way up the stairs, we see George stagger behind him, out of the room in which he killed Kathy and Joey.

The masked man starts calling C.J. by name as he makes his way up the stairs. The screen cuts to the young boy of George's nightmare on the same staircase, many years earlier. It's now apparent George knows who C.J. is, but we're not yet sure exactly how.

C.J. fires — and to my delight there really are no more bullets left in mom's revolver so he does what any good Daytona kid would do: runs into another room and removes a shotgun from a wall rack! Thank goodness this wasn't happening in a major city. *Thank God for southern gun laws circa 1981!*

C.J. runs into the hallway and blasts two holes into the masked man's midsection. It's kind of funny how C.J. stands perfectly still as he does this, but perhaps Bob or his mom had taken him to the range? (Not likely.) Either way, the masked man falls down the stairs and here, at 1:30:30, begins what I choose to call:

THE GRAND FINALE

This final sequence ranks among the most gruesome, disturbing, and horrifying ever to appear in a film. To this day the whole thing makes me cringe.

As George falls downstairs, we see flashbacks of a boy coming home from school. He takes his coat off and announces, "Hi dad, I'm home." Most children greet their mothers when arriving home, so keep that in mind for a forthcoming point.

The boy is dressed neatly in a white shirt with a black bowtie, giving the impression this is the 1950s or early 1960s. This picture of pure innocence is about to be destroyed beyond recognition.

The boy hears sounds coming from the second floor, and as he ascends the stairs to investigate, we notice it's the same staircase George Tatum has just fallen down. We realize we're about to see Tatum's full flashback, only hinted at throughout the film.

As young George approaches the master bedroom, we see a man — George's father — being tied to a bedpost by a woman in white lingerie, and while there has been some speculation as to whether this is George's mother or his father's mistress, I opt for the latter in view of the young George announcing his presence to his *father* on arriving home, rather than to both his mother and father. The father's reaction is also evidence this is not his wife.

The bedroom door is ajar, so it's easy for George to see what's happening. His father is restrained on the bed as the woman sits on his lap.

The camera slowly zooms into George's face as he watches the woman remove a white scarf/choker from her neck then begin to slap his father. The look on George's face is one of utter confusion (actor Scott Praetorius doesn't say a word yet conveys emotions the viewer can identify with).

Blood begins to drip from his father's nostrils as the woman smacks his face. George backs away from the room and quickly makes his way downstairs and then outside. The soundtrack loses the mellowness that began when young George arrived home; the sounds of chirping birds adds to the unease.

Young George makes his way to a shed. He opens the door and we see him standing in the entranceway as sun rays illuminate a barrel containing an axe — arguably the film's most crafted shot. Stills of it are as breathtaking as they are spooky. George takes his attention away from the barrel as he hears the smacking on the second floor. He looks up, as if he had doubted his *calling*, but emerges from the shed holding the axe in both hands. He begins the trek back upstairs as the soundtrack becomes manic.

The audience understands that George's father is enjoying the kinky sex play. Young George does not. We see the smile on George senior's face as his mistress ducks down to kiss him, revealing young George behind her at the foot of the bed, axe in hand.

When the woman sits back up, the boy swings the axe like a professional baseball player, cutting into her neck. Her blood splashes across his father's chest and face, and he screams his son's name over and over. The second whack is shown in slowmotion and we see the woman's head get cut clean off then fly onto the carpet.

The first time I saw NIGHTMARE the audience completely freaked out over this effect. Of course, having seen it countless times since, and despite the head being clearly fake, the effect is no less disturbing, especially when young George steps onto the bed and whacks the now headless corpse.

This he does eight times. His father screams "no!" repeatedly as blood is splashed on the walls and ceiling, creating a suburban slaughterhouse.

Young George finally slowly turns the axe toward his father, whose white shirt is now almost entirely red. He rests the axe between his father's eyes as he whispers something that sounds like either "Dad," or "Dead." George senior tries pleading with his crazed son, telling him he "Doesn't understand." But the boy slams the axe into his father's head, right between the eyes, and yes, while obvious the head is a dummy, the sound effects couple with the perpetrator being just a kid elevates the dread and terror to something altogether uncommon in slasher films.

The camera pans along the axe handle to young George's hands slowly releasing their grip. His face and clothing are covered in gore. When the camera cuts back to his father's head, blood is pouring out of it as if a dam had burst. Why the blood has taken so long to appear is one of the film's biggest FX criticisms, but the oozing audio effects make things as gross as they can get.

Young George then stares at himself in the blood-stained mirror. We know the boy has become psychologically damaged, yet his expression seems to be one of satisfaction, even accomplishment. Perhaps, considering how conservatively he is dressed, his father was a strict parent? Perhaps seeing his father in such a hypocritical position sent him over the edge?

George carefully steps off the bed, around the decapitated head on the floor, then takes a seat.

The film returns to the Temper house and the arrival at last of George Tatum's doctors, along with ambulances and cop cars. As the bodies of the babysitter and her boyfriend are carried out of the house on stretchers, C.J. looks on in horror with his mother and her boyfriend. When the EMT workers remove the mask from the killer, Susan screams, "No! That's my husband!" A crowd has formed around them.

C.J. is staring out of the back window of his parents car, directly at us. We see flashes of young George sitting at the scene of his crime all those years ago, raising his bloodied fingers to his mouth and taking a taste.

In the final shot of the film, the camera returns to C.J. He slowly smiles, then winks at us.

While NIGHTMARE never had a sequel (as of this writing there are rumors of a *prequel*), this ending ties in with most 1980s slasher films, making us believe C.J. has the same mental disorder as his father. I originally thought that having C.J. wink at the camera was silly, but perhaps his pranks throughout the film were more than just pranks? Perhaps he does have something in common with the father he never knew?

I'm amazed when I screen this film that so many people are genuinely surprised to discover the Tempers are George Tatum's

family. I don't recall being at all surprised by the revelation on my own initial viewing in 1982. Perhaps the film has aged better than I thought?

The credits roll with the same eerie but pleasant music used at the beginning of the film.

Final thoughts: NIGHTMARE is a flawed film. Yet despite its less than stellar acting and special effects, an interesting subplot that's barely mentioned let alone used to its full potential, and a few obvious plot holes, director Romano Scavolini has taken an ostensibly typical slasher trope and elevated it. The character of George Tatum is complex. He's a "real" killer, not a supernatural boogeyman who relies on wise cracks and cheap jump scares. While easily classified as a gore film (the film was a "video nasty" in the UK), NIGHTMARE's intense study of its mentally damaged lead gives the film its true chill factor. Baird Stafford's performance is grossly underrated, as he conveys much of his character by facial expressions alone. The same goes for actor Scott Praetorius, who, as the young George Tatum, conveys a variety of impressions without much dialogue. Critics can say all they want about the acting in this film, but Stafford and Praetorius shine and deliver unforgettable roles.

Because of the axe-mayhem finale, NIGHTMARE is often compared to THE SHINING, especially in light of George Tatum pick-axing his way through a door. Was

Scavolini inspired by Kubrick's masterpiece? Considering THE SHINING was a hit (the fourteenth biggest domestic grossing film of 1980), chances are he was influenced by it. FRIDAY THE 13th, also released in 1980 and another hit that year, also features a scene of an axe slamming into a head, portrayed with grim realism thanks to effects master Tom Savini. Axe murders are a staple of 1980s slasher films, but few were as effective or disturbing as the one in NIGHTMARE. Perhaps Scavolini wanted to better both THE SHINING and FRIDAY THE 13th combined? Either way, it is the most memorable and terrifying cinematic use of the weapon since 1972's SILENT NIGHT, BLOODY NIGHT.

As noted in my earlier book, Butcher Knives & Body Counts: Essays on the Formula, Frights, and Fun of the Slasher Film (Dark Scribe Press, 2011), I find that NIGHTMARE's use of children truly sets it apart from other slasher films. C.J. is stalked by this mysterious man — his father — as are his two sisters. They're in peril from the moment George Tatum is prematurely released from the mental hospital. Even when George is still miles away, there is a sense of unease whenever the kids are onscreen, be it during one of C.J.'s pranks or simply walking into the house after a day at school. Of course, C.J. carries most of the film; his sisters Tammy and Kim have little screen time, and his friend Tony only appears briefly before becoming a victim to Tatum. I give Scott Praetorius major props for his portrayal of the young George in what is arguably the most gruesome sequence a child actor has ever appeared in.

Although children in horror films was nothing new in 1981 — THE BAD SEED (1956), CHILDREN OF THE DAMNED (1964), and THE EXORCIST (1973) spring to mind — NIGHTMARE's use of them is on its own level, inasmuch as those films cited above are camp or use children in a supernatural context, NIGHTMARE puts them in a world all too real, all too believable. Unlike, say, 1974's DEVIL TIMES FIVE, a film in which sociopathic kids kill for no apparent reason, we believe George Tatum is triggered to murder by the kinky act he witnesses as a boy. And why, after the full flashback is revealed, the adult George Tatum can't stop killing.

We root for C.J. to defeat his father, which he does by entirely non-supernatural means, i.e. guns as opposed to holy water. C.J. may be a prankster but he sticks his neck out to ensure his sisters are safe. It's not often a film portrays kids in this type of situation and pull it off with little to no camp — admittedly, it requires some suspension of belief when C.J. fires a rifle as if he's a seasoned professional.

NIGHTMARE is a film that lives up to its title. While it is also known by many other titles (discussed later), I prefer the simple NIGHTMARE title best, as the film itself seems to unfold like a bizarre fever dream. George Tatum's nightmares run throughout, and while they're his nightmares, they can be considered real in the sense they are informed by what happened to him as a child. They become the viewer's nightmares, as we contemplate what it might be like to be him, or to be inside his mind.

"The Sheik," a mask made by the famous Don Post Studios, is worn by George Tatum in NIGHTMARE without the turban

TWO

THE CHARACTERS

In this section I'm going to look at every character in NIGHTMARE. I'm slapping the plain facts we know on the table, then will spend time speculating, especially about George Tatum, as the years between his childhood murder and adult killing spree are barely talked about in the film. I often spend too much time thinking about these characters and what they might be like outside of the film. Hence, some of my observations may seem funny, some way off (according to your own views), but either way I hope to bring this beloved cast *more to life* than you've ever thought possible.

Let's begin with what we know about **GEORGE TATUM**. It's not until the final minutes of the film that we discover what he did as a child, at an age I like to think was about twelve. We see him outside his suburban home on a cloudy day (and it *is* suburban; I don't

George Tatum (Baird Stafford)

recall houses spread apart like this in any city), making the neighborhood look gloomy, but it seems he grew up in a nice enough area. He lived with his father in a two-story detached house, complete with an outdoor shed. It bears repeating here that the woman George catches with his father in bed is *most likely* not his mother. You'd think if it was his mother she would've at least turned around or called his name. This woman does neither, so it is safe to assume she is a mistress or prostitute. For further proof, in one sequence, as George's two doctors are driving to Daytona, and one says that the police reports mention George's father and "the woman he was with." IMDb credits and Wikipedia be damned! Then again, in an interview with director Romano Scavolini on the Code Red Blu-ray edition of the film, he claims young George "kills his parents." But did Scavolini mean George had killed his mother at a separate time than during the films' infamous finale? I believe so: as mentioned in chapter one, when young George arrives home, he calls out to his *father* to announce his presence. Not once does he call out for his mother.

The act of violence George commits strongly suggests he had a pre-existing mental issue. To believe a twelve-year-old boy could suddenly snap to this extreme is a bit hard to swallow.

The last we see in the film of young George is him sitting in the corner of the room where he had just axe murdered his father and mistress, licking blood off his fingertips.

Who was George Tatum between this final scene as a boy and when we first meet him as an adult in a mental institution? Had he been arrested and placed in a juvenile detention center? Had he run away and somehow made it on his own? Even George's doctors don't seem to know much about his past, other than this violent incident at an early age.

We learn at the film's conclusion that the family he stalks and attempts to kill are his own wife and kids, suggesting that in his teen or late teen/early twenties, George managed to get his life together. Perhaps he was taken into custody and declared insane. Perhaps whatever juvenile program he was placed in worked well enough that authorities allowed him back into society. I'd love to know how George met his wife (who we will look at next) and what he told her about his past. Could it be possible George was still in touch with his mother, supposing she was still around at the time of his father's murder? Perhaps she vouched for him and raised him alone?

What we do know from the film about adult George: he's an intelligent man tormented by dreams of the murder he committed as a child. He speaks slowly but surely to the doctors in the institution and has

Susan Temper (Sharon Smith)

Bob Rosen (Mik Cribben)

little trouble getting from New York City to Florida via stolen cars. And when he realizes the experimental medication prescribed to him has stopped working, he calls his doctor from a motel room, an obvious plea for help.

We don't know what caused George, a married father of three children, to be institutionalized. One of George's psychologists claims he was committed after the murder of a *Brooklyn* family. Given that he killed his father in *Florida* as a child, we can assume Brooklyn happened in his adult life, shortly before the birth of his son C.J. Perhaps he was committed at his wife's suggestion, or maybe he had himself committed, worried he'd harm his family. It's interesting to note that George is in a secret, experimental drug program, one that if successful would see George used by the military or another secret agency. We can only wonder what it was George did for a living at the time of his marriage.

He lived with his family in Florida before being institutionalized, as he has little trouble finding them, and can creep around outside the house without being detected. George Tatum is a haunted, psychologically damaged man, yet evidently managed to get a solid education and support a family. Perhaps, if the rumored (in 2017) prequel to the film is ever made, we may find the answers.

SUSAN TEMPER, as we discover at the end of the film, is George Tatum's wife. She is the mother of a practical joker son, C.J., and daughters Tammy and Kim. She has a boyfriend, Bob, and always seems to be in a rush, although she's able to squeeze in private time with Bob aboard his boat and at social gatherings. She spends most of the film yelling at her son and trying to sell her house; she claims she has hated the place "Ever since the day he left, the day after C.J. was born," a knowing reference to her husband George. She seems to keep the kids in line, even with C.J.'s seemingly endless hi-jinks.

When Susan discovers it was her husband who almost killed her kids (and murdered her babysitter and boyfriend), she screams out, "That's my husband! It's my husband!" while

Man with Cigar (John Watkins)

Dr. Paul Williamson (Bill Milling)

holding her boyfriend's hand. Perhaps she wasn't sure if he'd ever get out of the institution? But the shock of seeing him also suggests she's surprised he's the killer, which makes us wonder just how much she knew about her husband's background, the violent tendencies or indeed the murder he committed as a child.

Being a busy mother of three, Susan no doubt went on anxiety medication after this grim discovery, but hopefully didn't mix it with the Scotch she was so fond of.

We assume Susan's boyfriend, **BOB ROSEN**, is some kind of hippie/slacker trust fund baby until Susan requires the services of the babysitter because of a "business party for Bob." It appears Bob lives on his yacht, which doubles as a getaway with Susan when the kids are in school. He's more than nice about Susan constantly running home to tend to her kids, and even provides the voice of reason when Susan freaks out over one of C.J.'s nastier pranks. At the drop of a dime, he'll suggest taking them all out for dinner, and we learn photography is his trade when he helps Susan take pictures of her home for the real estate agent.

We can assume Bob makes a decent living as a photographer, no easy feat in Florida in 1981. We're not sure if he's a homeowner, or just an artistic hipster content to live on the seas. And while C.J. never knew his real father, Bob is on his way to becoming a great stepdad, as evidenced when he spends a day with the family at the beach.

How can anyone not like this guy?

The head of the mental institution is known only as "**MAN WITH CIGAR**" in the film's credits. He's a slick talking, trench coat wearing boss to George's main therapist, Dr. Paul Williamson. He spends most of the film observing progress reports about George Tatum on a blurry computer screen, and when he learns Tatum was released prematurely, goes with Dr. Williamson to find him. Aggravated that Dr. Williamson has made a poor decision, he diligently works with him to help get George back into their care.

C.J. Temper (C.J. Cooke)

Kathy the Babysitter (Danny Ronan)

DR. PAUL WILLIAMSON, George Tatum's main doctor, seems perhaps a bit too easy-going considering he's dealing with a dangerous schizophrenic. But we know George likes to confide in him, as witnessed when George calls to say his urges are "Stronger than the pills." Dr. Williamson tries to reassure George that he is his friend but doesn't get much further with him.

Despite being called a "real schmuck" by his boss, Dr. Williamson seems focused and has no issue hopping on a plane to Florida in an attempt to locate his patient before another murder can be committed. Whether or not he still had a job at the institution after the killing spree is anyone's guess.

C.J. TEMPER is Susan's son with a love for practical jokes. He constantly tries to scare the hell out of his two sisters, and the family babysitter must be begged and bribed to come watch him. We know he never met his father, yet when C.J. first spots George lurking across the street from the house, we know he *senses* something.

C.J. likes to use ketchup for blood, is handy at making costumes out of Don Post Halloween masks and Christmas lights, and, like a typical kid, loves bike riding with his friends. Even with all his wise-ass habits, when he and his sisters are attacked by a masked madman in the film's final minutes, he protects them by holding the killer back with his mother's handgun (and shotgun). He may be a little crazy too, going back into the house to make sure the killer is dead.

Sure, C.J. is a genuine pain in the ass who may or may not have inherited his father's mental issues, but ultimately proves to be a hero to his sisters and his mother.

Aside from tattling on C.J., sisters **TAMMY** and **KIM TEMPER** are your average suburban schoolgirls who spend too much time watching television and not enough doing their homework. Living near the beach, we learn they like to eat fish and chips, and they never give their babysitter a hard time. They seem to love C.J. regardless of the constant pranks, although we're never sure of how they feel

about mom's boyfriend Bob. They're pretty much secondary characters, yet a vital component in what makes George Tatum tick…

KATHY is a blonde-haired babysitter who works for Susan Temper. She is fed up with C.J.'s antics and quits, but Susan convinces her to come back just one more time. She seems to be either a high school senior or college student, is attractive, and her boyfriend likes to sneak over to the Temper house when the kids are asleep.

Every slasher film from the early eighties needs a cute, tanned, sexually active female in the cast, and the stereotypical Kathy obliges by going outside to investigate noises and taking showers after shagging her boyfriend. We like that she returns to watch C.J. after Susan's pleading, although this last babysit proves fatal.

Her stoner boyfriend, **JOEY**, shows up in the final act to get laid, stoned, and strangled to death at the hands of a masked George Tatum. He's probably the guy you'd go to for weed in the parking lot before a concert. It seems the less we know about him, the better.

George's first victim as he travels down to Florida is **BARBARA**, a woman he stalks after seeing her in a roadside country/western bar.

Barbara (Kathleen Ferguson)

Telling her boyfriend **STEVE** she wants to be alone, she heads home from the bar after what has apparently been a rough day. Judging by her house and the way she dresses, Barbara is a professional type, most likely an office worker. While Steve tries to call to make sure she is okay, she is killed by George Tatum in one of the film's most grueling scenes.

CANDY is most likely one of the Temper's neighbors. Out jogging she says hello to C.J. as he passes on his bike, and when she later notices C.J.'s bike in front of an abandoned seaside house, goes inside looking for him (spoiler alert: this is a grave mistake). She falls victim to George and her body is discovered by C.J.'s friend **TONY**, before he too is murdered.

There are several other members of the cast in small roles. They include two sex workers at Times Square's Show World adult entertainment center, Susan's real estate agent (played by Ray Baker, who bears a striking resemblance to Ernest Borgnine), a third psychiatrist who joins our two doctors to hunt down George, a couple of orderlies and other workers at the mental institution, and a host of police officers.

THREE

AN INTERVIEW WITH KATHLEEN FERGUSON

The following interview took place on Monday, July 16, 2018, at a lovely park near Kathleen's home in Queens, NY. Being close to LaGuardia Airport, planes continually took off and flew overhead. But it was a beautiful day and during our conversation Kathleen paused a few times to show off her acting skills. Most memorable was her turn as Blanche from A STREETCAR NAMED DESIRE, which blew me away. A seasoned stage actress, Kathleen only starred in three feature films, my favorite being, of course, the role of Barbara in NIGHTMARE. She also worked with rescue dogs at 9/11 Ground Zero, was an international diplomat, and a belly dancer. Here, for the first time speaking publicly about the film, she shares some stories from the set, talks about her character Barbara, the woman from the bar scene who dies one of the most brutal deaths in the film and is George Tatum's first victim after leaving the institution. She also fondly remembers her early days as a stage actress.

Nick Cato: How did you get involved with NIGHTMARE? Was there a casting call?

KATHLEEN FERGUSON: I'm sure there was, but one of the producers was my boyfriend at the time. And I was offered a much bigger part, the part of the babysitter. But when I read through the script, I said nope! Not me, who was raised by nuns! I wasn't going to do these quasi-sex scenes and the bullshit when the boyfriend comes over. The worst I'll do is put on a towel and come out of the shower, so that's what they had me do. They were going to shoot me in the shower, but I was really uncomfortable with it, so I said, "Why don't you let the phone ring, and I'll come and answer it?" And they were fine with it. I didn't want to one day hear, "Hey grandma, why did you do that?" [laughs]

Tell us about your infamous kill sequence.

What they did was — you know those rubber things that go under dish drainers? They taped one over my body. Then the towel went on over it. So when the killer was stabbing me, when he was sitting on me and stabbing me, this was after he cuts my throat, he's supposed to be hitting the towel, because that's where the Rubbermaid protector is. He missed. [laughs] It was a retractable knife, *but* it hurt like hell!

Now this was the actor, Baird Stafford, doing this, not a stand in?

Yes! And he blew it and hit me on my ribs and I started to scream. They shot this… they decided to do it MOS* and then we'd do the screams in the studio. But I let out such a scream everyone was saying, "Why didn't we shoot this with the sound on?" And Baird is still chopping away at me, and I tried but couldn't get him off. I was really fighting him! And from the back I hear someone say, "Shouldn't we like… get her to a hospital or something?" and my boyfriend said, "No! This is great! Keep the camera rolling!" [laughs]

Your boyfriend was one of the producers, but also had a role, right?

Yes, he was one of the funnier characters. He was the psychiatrist with the white hair. Bill Milling.

Everyone I've ever spoken with about the film said the one scene that bothered them the most was the gurgling sound when you get your throat cut. Did you make those sounds?

Yes! That was me. I went into the studio, I was doing a lot of screams for a lot of characters. I got jobs on other horror movies doing screams, too. Wes Craven was a friend of ours. He came out with his 'Nightmare' series right after our NIGHTMARE. I think A NIGHTMARE ON ELM STREET came out two years after he saw our film. He started making it and of course he had a bigger budget than us.

But anyway, the NIGHTMARE crew had taken over this hotel down in Florida, the whole cast and crew were living there. Now, everyone is afraid of the special effects guys. I mean, they do the blood and gore and everything else. But every morning, I was the

* MOS is the term used when a scene is shot with no synchronous audio track.

AN INTERVIEW WITH KATHLEEN FERGUSON

Kathleen Ferguson with Nick Cato, 2018, Queens, NY, after Kathleen gave her first ever interview for this book.

Kathleen Ferguson in 2018.

one sent to wake these guys up! For some reason, the effects guys took a liking to me. I dunno… back then I was little, I was cute, y'know? So one day I knocked on the door and one guy answered and was like, "Oh, it's the kid again." So they invited me in for coffee, and all I see is intestines hanging from the drapery, which I learned they were making for another film. But their whole room was guts and all kinds of stuff hanging. Heads. Y'know. We'd sit in this room every day and eat breakfast together. You really become immune to this stuff!

But knowing these guys, they helped me out. They don't aim the stage blood at your face or things like that. They covered me good with stage blood during the stabbing scene, but there was so much, I think that's why Baird missed me with that retractable knife and hit my ribs. And Baird was really pounding down on me with that thing!

But in the studio, after trying a couple of times, someone came up with a solution to get my gurgling sound right for the throat slashing. I had asked what they were going to do, now that my vocal cords were cut, and they kept saying, "Don't worry about it… don't worry. It'll be fine." So I'm screaming my head off, on nano seconds on the editing screens so we can get everything timed right. Well, on screen my vocal cords get cut, and someone who had been standing behind me pulls my hair back, held my nose, and someone else threw a glass of water down my throat! [laughs]

Oh my God!

So, I was probably the first person in the United States to be waterboarded for the sake of art. [laughs] Then you get the [*Kathleen makes all kinds of crazy sounds*] trying to spit the water out. And I'm trying to gasp for breath and I'm spitting the water up and everyone around me is saying, "That's great!" I said, "Nice, but if you try doing it again, if you try a second take, now that I know what's coming, someone else is gonna be gurgling." [laughs]

You're a real trooper! I would've been swinging at people! You hear stories about "Scream Queens" but I've never heard anything even remotely like this. I'm assuming your boyfriend was watching this?

[Laughs] Oh yes! I think it was his idea! He was in the sound booth. I couldn't get the gurgly, disgusting sounds they wanted. Somebody pulls my hair back, pinches my nose, and throws a tumbler full of water down my throat. I was like, "They're drowning me!" Then I thought, "They're drowning me ... *for this picture*?" They better pay me a lot more!

What do you think would make them think you'd be cool with this? Were you known as the cool one on the set or something?

No, I think it's that they knew I was just starting out, they knew this was my first full length film, y'know. They knew I was young. They knew I didn't know about the union or union rules, they knew I wasn't a union member yet. Like Hitchcock said, "Actors should be treated like cattle." Well, I got the cattle prod that day.

Changing gears a bit... did you spend a lot of time working with Baird Stafford?

Oh, good Lord. That guy was *so* weird. I mean, weird in real life. I don't think he was acting in the film! He was so weird nobody would eat lunch with him. If we would have outdoor lunch, he'd be at a table *waaayyyy* over there, and the actors would be at one table, the techies would be at another, electrical department sat at that table ... but there was the killer all alone! All the actors were so afraid of him. I think if he would've come over to the actors table everyone would've got up and left. I think he did sit with the gaffers once.

What was it like working with Romano Scavolini as a director? Does he speak any English? Did he have a translator?

He did speak English on the set, but it was very garbled. He did have a translator. There were two directors and two producers. Remember that guy with the cigar in the film? He's the Executive Producer! This shows you how low budget this was. We had to cast from within. My boyfriend Bill was the line producer. We needed characters and we were like, "Who looks like a psychiatrist?" and everyone was like, "The guy with the white hair and the beard!" And of course, the money man was the Executive Producer, the guy with the cigar.

Would you mind telling us about the trunk incident?

[Laughs] After the psychopathic maniac cuts my

throat and stabs me a lot, he puts me in a garbage bag and throws me in the trunk of his car, and he drives to the beach to dispose of the body. So I'm wearing nothing but a heavy garbage bag when the killer puts me in the trunk, he puts me in there very sweetly, but once he slams the trunk closed, I hear a muffled [cry for] "LUNCH!" [laughs] And I'm waiting. And waiting. Nothing is happening! I'm waiting for someone to unlock the damn trunk and let me out. Then I'm banging on the trunk lid and screaming my head off. I said to myself, "They're trying to kill me. They are really trying to kill me!" Because this is Florida heat, the sun is beating down, and I'm sweating in this hot plastic bag. I'm only wearing this bag and my drawers! I keep banging and beating on the trunk, yelling for help and to let me out of there. Eventually I heard a *bam bam bam* on the trunk and someone said, "Shut up, you're supposed to be dead!" I told them, "Five more minutes and I *will* be. OPEN THIS DAMN THING!"

So they opened the trunk and I kind of crawled out. I was *soaked*. So I said, "You guys all enjoy your lunch?" I must've lost ten pounds in there. I told them, "Now I am going to lunch," and they complained that I'd be holding up the picture. I told them they didn't need me until Baird carries me onto the beach, and that I was going to eat and *they* were going to pay for it! I told them I was going to order five lunches for what you SOBs did to me. They told me there was a No Shirt, No Shoes policy down at the IHOP [restaurant chain International House of

Pancakes] where they'd had lunch, and I said, "Wanna see me?" So I borrowed sneakers off the make-up lady, punched my arms through the garbage bag, then I borrowed a belt from someone, and the crew finally understood my temper. In fact, the special effects guys threatened to strangle everyone with fake intestines if someone didn't lend me a belt! So I tied the belt around the bag and made it look as much like a dress as I could. So I went to the IHOP about half a mile down the road, had lunch on the movie's tab, then came back and realized I had sweated all my make-up off. I had mascara lines running down my face when I entered the IHOP because one of the waitresses said to me, "Madam, would you care to wash your face?" [laughs] And I did. I had washed everything off. So now back on the set I was looking at another hour and a half in the make-up chair.

How long were you actually in that trunk until they let you out?

Well, they took an hour for lunch, then however long it took them to run errands, go to the hardware store, whatever. It had to be at least two hours.

Between this and the waterboard story you should've been the highest paid actress on the planet!

You'd think so, right?

Were you on the set for scenes other than yours?

Oh yeah. I was very involved with a lot of the backstage stuff. I did hair on some of the other actors, lots of stuff. Oh… and I ran into an old friend, Frank, from high school, who had moved down to Florida! Right after graduation he had gone down to Florida for college. So we met up and he took me to lunch and was insisting I tried the crawfish. He wanted to hear all about the film I was there working on. So we had lunch, it was really nice to see Frank again, and what really made me cry was when he said, "I can't believe you're *really* doing it." He knew this had been my dream since I was a kid. He knew everyone was telling me in high school that this was impossible, it was too hard… but here I was. So, of course I asked him if he wanted to come back to the set, and he did, so I gave him a tour of who was doing what, the different departments. The first place I took him was to my friends in the special effects department with the intestines hanging off their curtains. Occasionally, if those guys wanted to be left alone, they'd leave the door to their studio partially open with a bucket of stage blood on the top, y'know that old college trick. They usually did that if they didn't want to be bothered with anyone when they were working on something. You could see why everyone was afraid of those guys! But they were very talented. They'd argue over how realistic a liver or something looked: "Hey, maybe that needs a little bit more fat on one side?"

There was a lot of controversy around the effects, as a few different guys were credited with them. I know Ed French and Cleve Hall were onboard.

Yes, yes. Hey, I even spit in the paint!

Do you know anything about the Tom Savini thing?

Yes! There were *so* many people on this film who helped and advised. So much so that it got confused as to who actually did some of the special effects. I know Tom Savini came in and gave some advice, I think he worked one day with the guys. Maybe two. I'm not sure because it wasn't a day that I worked.

I know he won a lawsuit for using his name as the main special effects guy.

Oh yeah. Yep. Y'know, you can't *walk by* a movie set if you're famous without people saying you were there. There was a story from years ago where Ethel Barrymore showed up in the background on some film and she wound up getting the main acting credit!

NIGHTMARE came out in 1981. I didn't get to see it until a year or two later on a double feature with MOTHER'S DAY. Did you get to see it on its initial release in New York City?

Many times! We got the entire cast together and we would go to different neighborhoods to see what the reaction was like. And, there were some neighborhoods where the people yelled back at the screen: "Don't go up the stairs! He's waiting for you!" [laughs] One day people were yelling at the screen louder than you could hear the dialogue! So Bill [Milling] said, in the theater, "Everybody stand up and just turn around and say 'Shhhhh!'" So we all did, we put our fingers in front of our lips and said, "Shhhh!" I heard one guy say, "Oh my god IT'S THEM!" [laughs] "And she's not dead," he said pointing to me! "And she's not dead," he said, pointing to someone else. Someone else pointed at Bill and said, "It's the stupid psychiatrist!" [laughs]

Yeah, Bill and the cigar guy were funny.

But they hated each other in real life! That's why it worked! Cigar man calls Bill a schmuck… that wasn't really acting.

Did you also get to see it in Times Square?

Yup. We did. And *that* was fun. You had a totally different crowd there.

It was always very lively there when I used to go.

Yep. I haven't been back there since they Disneyfied the place. I remember when it had all the girly slot machines, like they showed in our movie. I miss walking around there and seeing the porn film marquees that had the clever, funny titles! They would have these titles and bylines like "He shoots to conquer!" [laughs] They'd take these classic plays and just mess them up. I saw one marquee where they did KEY LARGO, but as a porn film. [laughs] And NIGHTMARE was shot, I was told, exactly like a porn film. I heard most horror films are shot the same way too. You have a little bit of story, then what they call a "commercial scene." In a porn film that's sex, in a horror film it's blood and gore and murders and all kinds of tricks going on. Then you have a little more plot. [laughs] In our film you had those two on the sailboat, then the kid with the ketchup trying to trick everyone. [laughs] Then another murder. It's the same thing in porn but with sex. Unless you're making a history film, these "commercial scenes" are why people are paying for their ticket. Whether they want to see porn, horror, dancing penguins, whatever.

Did you get to spend any time with C.J. Cooke, the kid who kept pranking everyone? When NIGHTMARE came out, one of the TV ads said, "Introducing C.J. Cooke!" like they thought he was going to be the next big child star.

They tried. And I think his mother insisted on that TV ad thing. But, uh, that kid was going nowhere. [laughs] I'm sorry! Well NIGHTMARE was his only appearance. Maybe his mom sent him for acting lessons? Maybe he did a couple of school plays but that was about it. I don't know because I didn't follow him.

I was always fascinated with C.J. and the actor who plays the young George Tatum. The film is very brutal. Even as a horror fan, I always wondered how the parents were convinced to let their children do these roles.

Well, if you look at how the film is edited, look at the scene with young George [Scott Praetorius]. He opens the door, and he's holding a hatchet. And then the next shot is looking at dad tied to the bed with the mistress on top of him. Young George, the

actor, isn't seeing that on the set. All he sees is he's opening a door. And he's holding a hatchet. Kids *love* to play with fake hatchets. [laughs] So then they say to the kid, "Look pissed off," or whatever they said to make him look mad. Then the actor makes a face, then between takes they splatter a little blood on him, and so on ... I mean, did you ever really look at the hands that wielded that axe? How big were those hands? [laughs] Y'know? So, that kid saw nothing as they filmed this. He opened the door. He ran up and down the stairs to get the hatchet. He held up the hatchet. And he looked surprised. And during this they gradually put red stage blood on him. We, the audience, see everything but that kid didn't. We do not abuse children in film.

But I'm sure the parents were told what the final scene would look like?

[laughs]

Who were the actors, or films, that made you want to get into acting?

Oh there were a lot. I really admired Katherine Hepburn. Greta Garbo, in a scene from QUEEN CHRISTINA, where she's looking out over the boat, and it looks like she has all the wisdom of the ages on her face? The director had told her, "Just stand there and think of *nothing*." When I heard that I thought, "That's brilliant," because he got the look he wanted. Luise Rainer is one of my favorites. She did THE

GOOD EARTH. A German actress. She convinced the filmmakers to give her more dialogue, as women weren't allowed to talk all that much back then.

What was one of your earliest roles?

I played Juliet when I was fifteen, at St. Kevin's. And for all of my friends who remember that, *please* forget it. [laughs] There was a guy who played Friar Lawrence who misunderstood his lines. He flubbed one line so bad that for *years* he was sick of people coming up to him and reciting his misread dialogue! [laughs] But I had had some training at this point. The Franco Zeffirelli film came out in 1968. We did our play in '69. I had a long red velvet dress and hair down to my waist. I think I was a perfect Juliet! We did the death scene in the charnel house and Romeo tried to be dead without laughing! Try being a teenager and pull that off!

What was one of your favorite roles?

I did Juliet again as an adult, the whole play, and I loved it. I really loved it. I worked with the local college here doing costumes and make-up, and they couldn't find a part for me. Then again, I wasn't even enrolled in a class. [laughs] But they liked having a pro hanging around, and because this was the most difficult part, I ended up getting it. I thank an old acting coach for that. I had taken his advice to heart.

But my absolute favorite character to play was Blanche DuBois from A STREETCAR NAMED DESIRE. [*At this point, Kathleen paused from our interview to give me an impromptu performance from STREETCAR, and it simply blew me away. I was teary eyed by the end of it, and she grabbed my wrist and thanked me for my attention.*] I actually did that one scene from STREETCAR for several psychiatrists … who *believed me*.

I just believed you!

[laughs] Thanks. I did it for my ex-husband, and even *he* believed me! I was trying to teach him (as he had only done musicals, which only had a couple of lines) that you had to bring acting down to a conversational level. I asked him to ask me about an ex-boyfriend. He did, then I launched into the scene from STREETCAR. And he believed I wasn't acting! [laughs] He didn't believe it until I showed him the page from the script where I got the dialogue from! He said to me, "I didn't know if I should call the police or the loony bin!" [laughs]

NIGHTMARE has developed a cult following, mainly due to its video releases. Have you met with fans over the years?

No! You're the first person! I had no idea anyone had any interest in it. I thought this film was a "make a quick buck and go on to the next picture" thing.

I'm shocked no one ever contacted you, especially with the two Code Red releases of the film. They featured interviews with Baird, some effects guys, Mik Cribben…

Mik Cribben? (blows loud raspberry) No comment.

Well, the film wasn't well received at first. Janet Maslin ripped it apart in her *New York Times* review the day it opened.

I know! We hung it up in the office!

The film follows a typical slasher film pattern, but to me, and a legion of fans, there's just *something* about it. It's very eerie. It's just so nihilistic.

[laughs] Well, the film doesn't care about *anybody*. Even when she [Sharon Smith] screams at the end, "It's my husband! It's my husband!" they just go to the newsman: "Well, this is Ralph Miller with WKXY, and..." [laughs] It just... it had no emotional closure, and it really had no emotional opening. Even the psychiatrist was like "Oh, it's only a dream George, and dreams can't hurt you." [laughs] Blah blah blah! And they didn't care what was happening to this guy! Imagine how George felt.

Did you get to meet Sharon Smith, who plays the mother in the film?

Oh yes. She was a really nice lady. She was very professional. And if she could stand Mik hanging all over her... [laughs] She was very professional and always knew her lines, knew where to stand, and had no trouble with anything. Some characters were a little loopy, they'd show up late, or hungover, y'know? Not her.

Have you stayed in touch with anyone from the film?

I haven't seen anybody from the film since... I'm in touch with Bill online on occasion. He married a psychologist which I think was very good for him. [makes funny face]

People connected to this film are hard to get in touch with. That's why when the Code Red DVD came out a lot of fans were surprised. A lot of people never did interviews for horror magazines over the years.

Well, a lot of them got out of the business. Some had kids. Oh... just remembered! One of the other producers wanted to be in the movie, too... he's the bartender! Everyone wants to be in the movies! Bill was the line producer, Cigar Man was the executive producer, who felt like we were pissing too much money away faster than we should have. They both acted in the film. One of the reasons those two fought all the time!

When I saw a screening of the film last summer in Brooklyn [July 2017], a lot of younger people in attendance seemed taken aback that Cigar Man had a cigar in his mouth in the hospital!

[laughs] Yes! Well in the eighties people could smoke in the hospital, they could smoke almost anywhere.

What horror films, if any, were you a fan of before starring in NIGHTMARE?

Oh, the Dracula films. I love the vampires. Bela Lugosi was the first sex symbol I think I ever had! Even when I was only eight! I mean, here's this elegant, older man ... I was done! There's

AN INTERVIEW WITH KATHLEEN FERGUSON

Kathleen Ferguson with Nick Cato (2018)

a lot of innuendo with vampire films, with all the bodily fluids going into each other, the being bit four times thing, y'know. As secret as sex was back when *Dracula* was written, it was very sexual. I also love the Vincent Price film THEATER OF BLOOD, where he kills off people in Shakespearean ways. So good! It's a real actor's film.

Thank you so much for your time, Kathleen! I know the legion of NIGHTMARE fans appreciate it, too.

I miss all the actors, the business in general. I had so much fun talking about this. Thank you so much.

FOUR

AN INTERVIEW WITH PRODUCER BILL MILLING

The following interview took place on January 25, 2023. Bill Milling is the producer of the NBC series UNICORN TALES, winner of eighteen Emmy Awards, and the prestigious Action for Children's Television Award. He is also the writer/director of over twenty feature films, and early in his career was involved with NIGHTMARE.

Bill Milling not only co-produced NIGHTMARE but also played the pivotal role of Dr. Paul Williamson in the film, the psychiatrist who prematurely releases George Tatum from the mental institution. Bill took time from his busy schedule to speak with me.

Nick Cato: How did you get involved with director Romano Scavolini? Did you know him before this film?

Bill Milling: No, he was introduced to me through a young man who was working for me, and then I brought him into August Films, where I was working, and then I introduced him to the staff there. We got the film funded through Goldmine Productions, who put up the money. So, the man who worked for me on one of my films was a PA, who ended up becoming a producer. He brought NIGHTMARE to me, and I brought it into August Films.

So as producer, was your main role dealing with the financing?

I was actually a *line* producer. My job was really bringing together the crew, the equipment, the cameras, the logistics... the basic line producer functions.

Did you bring in or suggest any of the actors?

Well, the actress who dies after she gets out of the shower, Kathleen Ferguson, who at that point was my girlfriend, and Mik Cribben, who was the still photographer, he turned out to be one of the actors. Of course, Romano pulled me in to be one of the actors. My part was supposed to be very, very small, and then it kept growing and growing as the film went on. Romano's people, in my estimation, chose actors based on their *look* rather than any acting abilities, because he cast them before actually auditioning anyone with any kind of a reading.

Now, the *girl in the shower* is the *girl in the shower*, a trope in these kinds of movies, but it turned out that Mik Cribben actually was an actor. He was a friend of mine. So, his role turned out alright. I had done a bunch of acting, so that turned out alright. But the basic casting of the film didn't go through the ordinary, rigorous casting process. It was more like Romano looked at someone, and he felt that person looked good for the part.

We shot NIGHTMARE in twenty-one straight days, in a house in Florida. Twelve-hour days. We drove down from New York, me and the crew, in a bunch of rickety vans. We were two people to a van loaded with all the gear. The whole reason we decided to shoot in Florida was to be on the beach near Cape Canaveral when the rocket took off, and we finally shot it, but it never made it into the movie. That was very bizarre.

I was also the primary special effects director on the film. I know Tom Savini was given credit, and it's possible he did something *after* the film was shot, that was cut into the film, that I never saw. But all that business with the arm being ice-picked on the table, *I* did all that. Everything on set, I was the only special effects person down there for the twenty-one days of the shoot. I'm uncredited, not that I care because I'm not a special effects person.

I understand the flashback sequence with young George killing his father and mistress was shot in my hometown of Staten Island?

That is *probably* true. That was done after we finished filming in Florida. I didn't have anything to do with that scene.

On the Code Red DVD there's an interview with special effects artist Ed French, who took credit for that sequence.

He probably did! I knew Ed French. He's an

actual effects artist who I've worked with. He probably did that, that's probably accurate. I don't know what Tom Savini could've done.

I met Savini at a 1985 Fangoria convention. He said he was on the set one day just to give pointers. Kathleen Ferguson said she saw him on the set, too.

Huh. I knew who Savini was. So, if he was on set, that's strange I didn't see him.

Can you share anything about the child actors, in particular Scott Praetorious who plays the young George Tatum? I located a man online who claimed to be him, but he vanished after I emailed him some interview questions which he had agreed to do for this book.

You know, I don't know anything about him. I wasn't involved with that flashback sequence.

There is a video company who have been claiming they have a scene of CJ's friend Tony hanging from a noose in the boathouse scene. A still of this even showed up online a few years ago. Are you aware of this or any other scenes that may have been cut or lost?

Wow! I'm not aware of this scene at all, no.

I'll tell you this: my main memories were

Bill Milling today

that drive down to Florida, and I did a lot of work on it every day, but we did have a *lot* of fun. The whole crew did. You'd think twenty-one straight days of twelve-hour shoots would be grueling, but because we stayed in a motel right down the block from the house we filmed in, it was no big deal. So, you know, you film twelve hours, you sleep eight, then you still have time to go do some other stuff. We were a pretty happy family. There was not a lot of tension on the crew, and we all enjoyed it.

I don't think the film is a masterpiece, by any means, but it is a fun one.

Can you tell us what you do today?

I own the American Movie Company. We represent some thirty studios in New York City. We're a film and television producing company. We own all our own cameras; we have our own crew. We also do webcasting. We're the largest teleprompter company in North America. We do some high-end visual effects, XR virtual reality motion capture, all those things. Our website tells you everything else we do.

Good luck on your future endeavors and I'm sure NIGHTMARE fans around the world appreciate you talking with us.

Thank you, my friend. Thank you so much!

FIVE

GEORGE TATUM'S KILL SCENES

Love or hate NIGHTMARE, one thing that can't be denied is that it's gruesome, and whether one finds the special effects believable or not isn't the point: in 1970, the 'godfather of gore' Herschell Gordon Lewis delivered one of his goriest films (THE WIZARD OF GORE), and while most of the FX look terrible, over a half-century later the film still manages to disgust.

For a slasher film with such a low body count, NIGHTMARE's reputation as a bloodbath lives up to the hype. This brief chapter revisits some things discussed earlier, but a film with such notorious standing in the horror community demands a chapter devoted to the kills.

Some of NIGHTMARE's special effects work fine, and some not so much — especially after repeat viewings. But even when it's apparent you're looking at a dummy or a close-up of a sheet of latex, the sound effects and general tone of the film still make these scenes effective.

While there are flashbacks of a violent murder throughout the film (revealed in full in the finale), the first victim George murders onscreen is Barbara (Kathleen Ferguson; see previous chapter for a behind the scenes look at this sequence). After following her home from a bar in South Carolina, George waits for her to get out of the shower, sneaks up behind her as she answers a phone call, then slashes her throat with a kitchen knife. While throat slashings have been seen in countless films, it's the extreme close-up that makes this one so grim. And as mentioned in the first chapter, the gurgling audio effects make it difficult to palate.

Not satisfied, Tatum lets her body fall to the carpet and then sits on her legs as he proceeds to stab her abdomen, slowly, repeatedly, the anguish on his face mirroring his internal struggle. When he's done, Tatum is in tears and apologizes to his victim, who could've been anyone, which makes the scene spooky even on top of all the bloodshed.

The next two murders happen off screen, but we see the aftermath of one. Candy, a neighbor of CJ, is killed in an abandoned waterfront house. Tatum then kills CJ's young friend Tony, who also comes looking for him. Before he dies, he sees Candy seated in a chair, bloody, with a rat crawling on her shoulder. I hadn't seen any version that shows Tatum killing Tony, until the Severin 4K cut of the film which came out in 2023. There is a quick cut of Tatum apparently about to strangle Tony. I'm sure censors would've been more upset over that than any other scene in the film.

The next victim is Joe, the Babysitter's stoner boyfriend. As he smokes a joint waiting for Kathy to get out of the shower, a masked Tatum strangles him with a wire. When Kathy returns in a bathrobe with a towel on her head, she spots the masked figure and thinks it's CJ pulling another prank, having worn the same mask earlier. But as she goes to call CJ's mother, Tatum uses a small pickaxe to nail her arm to the table. Her bathrobe opens, exposing her back. Tatum then whacks her several times, with slow close ups of the pickaxe making holes up and down her back. This sequence is particularly nasty, especially when we discover young CJ has witnessed much of the murder.

While protecting his two sisters from the intruder, CJ puts a few bullets into Tatum with a handgun, then blows him down the stairs with a rifle. As he lays bleeding and dying, we're finally shown the gruesome murder Tatum committed as a child, hitherto only hinted at in snippets.

After witnessing his father tied to a bed and slapped by a mistress, George goes out into the shed and grabs an axe. He returns to his father's bedroom and strikes the mistress once in the neck, causing a gush of blood. After a second strike, her head is knocked off and flies through the air. It's an obvious prop, but the quick close-up shot of the woman's hands feeling the decapitated neck still causes goosebumps in this viewer. Young George then steps atop the bed and strikes the decapitated body several more times, causing blood to splash around the room and cover his father's face.

George then rests the axe between his father's eyes, ignores his pleads, and brings the blade crashing down. The force causes the whole bed to sink down, shown in slow motion. After a long shot of the father with the axe handle sticking out from his head, we see a close-up of blood gushing out. I don't know why it was decided to show this several moments after the axe enters the man's skull, but it's quite gross if a bit oddly timed.

One gruesome throat slashing and multiple body stabbings. Two off screen murders. A brutal strangulation. A violent pick-axe attack. The barbaric double axe murder of a man and his mistress at the hands of a *child*. These seven

murders (five of which are graphically shown) resulted in NIGHTMARE being labelled a 'video nasty' and banned in its original uncut form, while also making it one of the most notorious slasher films of the 1980s, if not all time.

The late great Chas Balun had this to say about the film's plot and FX:

"Another Halloween-ish rip-off although done with some degree of skill and cunning. A similar formula of a child witnessing a terrifying murder only to have it haunt him years later. What it lacks in originality it makes up for in explicitly gruesome, convincing effects which leave nothing to the imagination. Especially noteworthy is the unbearably realistic hunting axe in the face that manages to gag you and fascinate you with its thoroughness. I've never quite been able to figure out how these micro-budget horror-schlocko movies come up with such outstanding effects. Some, not all, of the effects in NIGHTMARE are on a level with Savini, Fullerton or Burman and what seems even more amazing is the quantity of effects in these films.

"Not as bad as one might imagine, but only for hardcore splatter aficionados."*

* Chas Balun, *The Connosseuir's Guide to the Contemporary Horror Film* (Fantaco, 1983).

SIX

DVD / BLU-RAY REVIEWS

CODE RED

From 2010 to 2018, I wrote a column for a website called Cinema Knife Fight*. In 2011 the site's owner asked me if I'd review the just-released Code Red DVD of NIGHTMARE knowing I was a big fan. The Code Red DVD was the first major release in the USA of the film since it's two previous releases on VHS, which were from Planet Video in 1982, then from Continental Video in 1985. If you didn't have access to one of these VHS releases, the only way to view the film until Code Red's DVD was on poorly uploaded YouTube posts, which were often quickly taken down. What follows is the review as it appeared on the site. The Blu-ray was still a year or two away. I've addressed some points with comments as highlighted. (It should also be noted that in the UK, NIGHTMARE was released unauthorized on video in 1982 and 1984 (most notably by

* Cinema Knife Fight closed in 2018 after publishing daily film reviews for over ten years.

World of Video 2000), which led to lawsuits as the film was on the 'video nasties' list, but it was finally given an official video certificate in 2002. It wasn't until 2016 when a proper DVD release finally came to the UK thanks to video company 88 Films).

FINALLY! The wait is OVER…

Most (if not all) of my faithful readers are sick and tired of hearing me go on about the 1981 slasher film NIGHTMARE (a.k.a. NIGHTMARES IN A DAMAGED BRAIN). I've been telling people about it since 1982, when I first saw it on a double bill with MOTHER'S DAY (1980), and I've had countless family members and friends sit through my well-worn VHS copy over the years. And yet despite the digital video uprising, a proper DVD had not been released in America (those with turbo-DVD players had the option to buy a British DVD that has been on the market for several years). Enter Code Red DVD, a specialty DVD company who release deluxe editions of rare and seldom-seen horror, action, and comedy films. Since 2007, Code Red had been promising a DVD of NIGHTMARE, and due to too many factors to discuss here, it was continually placed on their back burner. We die-hard fans visited Code Red's blog nearly every day, awaiting word, and were occasionally teased with pictures and info of the coming DVD extras.

AT LONG LAST: on July 26th of this year, NIGHTMARE was finally released in a 2-disc package that has already become as controversial as the film itself (sorry about the plug, but for a full review of the film, see my chapter in the book BUTCHER KNIVES AND BODY COUNTS— to be released shortly from Dark Scribe Press).

Before I get to the DVD review, newcomers should know that NIGHTMARE is pretty much a generic slasher film. It's low budget and features some less than stellar acting. But what set NIGHTMARE apart from other "psycho-leaves-nuthouse-too-early" films are its grueling tone, its over-the-top splatter scenes, and an amazing performance by star Baird Stafford, who portrays George Tatum, a killer haunted by a vicious murder he committed at a young age.

NIGHTMARE instantly made the UK's "Video Nasty" list, and there was much controversy over who was responsible for the disgusting special effects (there's a few extras on this DVD that deal with the Tom Savini-issue … if you haven't heard about this, Google it — or better yet, get the DVD).

Before I sat down to review this DVD, I read

what some fans were saying about it and was surprised to see so much arguing. Some praised the three (yep — three!) transfers of the film included here, while others claim Code Red did a sloppy job with all of them. I watched the entire film in its newest transfer (a 2011 telecine), which looked fine to me. I then scanned through certain scenes on the 2008 high-definition transfer and the 2005 "corrected telecine transfer approved by director Romano Scavolini." To be honest, there are differences, but I'm not one of those VIDEO WATCHDOG anal-retentive film inspectors who spends countless hours deciding if someone's toe made it into a certain frame or not: to me they ALL look good, and I'm just happy to have this film preserved on a digital edition (hence, if YOU'RE an anal-retentive DVD freak, go check out the arguments happening on Amazon.com and various message boards. Life's too short for this nonsense, in my opinion).

[Note: My comment above about VIDEO WATCHDOG wasn't a mock or a shot at Tim Lucas' magazine. I've read it from the first issue and loved it. Tim often brings points to light about film transfers that are crucial. That said, there are way too many people, in the case of NIGHTMARE, who I think have made too much of an issue over these film transfers. There are plenty of online blogs you can seek out if this is your thing.]

The DVD itself is a lot of fun: the main menu boards feature moving scenes from the film (although I thought it was a bit too spoiler-ish to show the intense finale on one of these) and each board is easy to navigate (as far as I know there are no Easter Eggs here). Among the extras is a VERY informative audio commentary with star Baird Stafford and make-up effects man Cleve Hall. There's a nice making-of feature with more from Stafford and Hall, as well as ex-distributor Tom Ward. But perhaps the most sought after extra here is an interview with special effects maestro Ed French, who gives his side of the Tom Savini story (again, Google this if you're interested). It's a bit short, but good. There are also two NIGHTMARE trailers, one that I hadn't seen before.

NOW, where Code Red has annoyed some fans: While it's true that we NIGHTMAREians have haunted Code Red to release this film for years, one of the main reasons (besides financial) was the inability to have a 90-minute interview with the director translated and/or subtitled. Yet the interview is included here in Italian – I'm assuming Code Red did this to break our chops (and after you see the sarcastic blurbs and synopsis they've placed on the front and back of the DVD case, you just might agree). I'm guessing those who aren't die-hard fans of the film might get pissed off over this … personally, I found it funny. TRUE, I'd like to hear what Romano Scavolini has to say, but I guess I'll have to wait until I can convince my grandmother to come over and translate for me…

[NOTE: The Code Red Blu-ray edition has the Scavolini interview with English subtitles. My grandmother got off easy! Since writing the review, I've read claims online that the interview had not been translated at the time of the DVD because of the cost in so doing. Whether true is anyone's guess, but either way it was a real treat to finally "hear" what Scavolini had to say in such a lengthy interview.]

Was the wait for this DVD worth it? For me, while someone could've released it without all the extras and I'd still be happy, having the commentaries and especially the

making-of feature was WELL worth the wait. And although I actually heard Tom Savini speak about the film at a 1985 FANGORIA convention about his involvement, it was nice to hear two other sides of the story (and all three basically mesh).

If you have a cast iron stomach and want to see a gore film that's genuinely spooky at times, give NIGHTMARE a shot; aside from the first EVIL DEAD (1982), it's one of those rare horror films where the splatter actually ADDED to the chills and caused a disturbing atmosphere. I also believe any serious horror film DVD collector should have this seldom-seen gem in their collection (while they still can).

Now let me see what grandma is up to…

[NOTE: Neither the Code Red DVD or Blu-ray are presently available from Code Red but used copies can be found elsewhere with prices ranging up to and over $100.]

WHAT OTHERS HAVE SAID ABOUT THE CODE RED DVD/BLU-RAY RELEASE:

Fans of the film grabbed the Code Red DVD and basically slobbered all over it, myself included. Contextualising the significance of

this release for fans, here are some comments that appeared on various film blogs. They appear with the blessing of the respective authors. Check out the complete reviews online at your leisure.

"The 2-disc set is packed with extras as well as three different cuts of the film to choose from. Considering it took so long for this movie to finally surface on DVD, its release was just as problematic as all the other problems surrounding the movie itself. In a bid to both please and piss off its fan base, Code Red has populated this set with a playfully bitter sense of humor—such as including a 95-minute interview with Romano Scavolini in Italian WITHOUT English subtitles. Not only that, but the second disc sporting the superior print has a label that looks like a bootlegger's DVD-R!

"The turmoil surrounding the compilation and inclusion of this interview is no doubt a reflection of the love/hate relationship CR has with its relatively small buying market. Fans of these niche titles can be fickle and difficult to please, but both giving them the product and giving them the finger isn't the most logical, nor mature thing to do. Still, it's great to have the movie on the shiny disc as well as the other extras including interviews and commentary."

—Excerpt from a review by VENOM5 on *Cool Ass Cinema*

"Now we jump forward to 2014 with something that had to be coming sooner or later, a Blu-ray edition from Code Red. The transfer is advertised as a brand new 2013 master, which means you're getting a nice HD upgrade of that superior third option. The boost in resolution helps, not surprisingly, with detail sharpening up and the plentiful shades of red benefiting from better color reproduction. This probably won't ever look like its slicker fellow slashers due to the nature of its production, but fans should be pleased with the results. Damage is very minimal here, with a fleeting green scratch in the opening scene and a few flecks here and there. The DTS-HD mono audio sounds solid as well. As for extras, you get the Stafford/Hall/Christian/DeCoteau commentary, the making-of featurette, the long version of the theatrical trailer, the Ed French featurette, and in a nice touch, the Scavolini interview with - yes! - English subtitles at last ("subtitled by cult icon Damon Packard"). On top of that there are also two new interviews, starting with an 8-minute featurette with producer Bill Milling (who stepped in front of the camera to play the bearded psychiatrist). He goes over the grueling 12-day shoot without breaks, the reason his part kept getting bigger, and the fun working habits of Scavolini on the set. Then there's a new 11-minute interview with Mik Cribben, who worked as the unit production manager and wound up stepping in as the bandanna-wearing, ostensible good guy in the film. Once again, it's a fun, candid perspective on the film covering tension between Scavolini and the producers, the Florida shooting, acting in his skivvies, backstage drama with people getting shuffled around and fired, and a somewhat jumbled account of the whole poster controversy.

"In late 2015, UK label 88 FILMS threw an interesting twist into the story of this film's video history with its separate Blu-ray and DVD releases as number 12 in its Slasher Classics Collection. The BBFC brouhaha long gone, the film was free to pass uncut -- and in a slightly longer version previously unseen on home video, clocking in at 99 minutes (about 39 seconds longer than the complete US cut on the Code Red disc). This doesn't consist of gore, but random bits of scene extensions confined to the first third of the film, mainly bits at the heads and tails of scenes presumably lost due to element damage or removed for pacing reasons. The color timing is radically different here, looking brighter and cooler with more detail visible but whites also tended to bloom more; The 88 FILMS transfer has a slight bit of extra info at the bottom of the frame, which means the already eyebrow-raising bit with the vibrator in the peepshow now reveals even more. The LPCM English mono soundtrack has been cleaned up quite a bit but features some pretty extreme leaps in volume, so be prepared to have your remote handy or any nearby pets or neighbors might get very upset. Extras here are completely different, so to put it simply, slasher films will simply want to have both releases in their collections. Associate producer Bill Paul provides a new audio commentary about working with the Italian director, handling the location shifts between New York and Florida, and coordinating the very messy gore effects with the occasional participation of child actors; it's a solid alternate history compared to the older one. A brief three-minute interview with 21st CENTURY FILMS CEO Tom Ward is a thumbnail sketch of the film's controversial theatrical release in the US with bit about the special effects dispute, and "Terror in Times Square" features former FANGORIA editors Mike Gingold and Tony Timpone guiding you through the radically changed areas where the opening scenes were shot. Scavolini and Stafford are covered in the insert booklet via print interviews."

—Excerpt from a review by Nathaniel Thompson on mondo-digital.com

MASSACRE VIDEO

Shortly after I began writing this book, a company called Massacre Video promised an all new 2K restoration on Blu-ray. According to their website, "Previous disc releases have utilized a worn 35mm release print or an uncorrected answer print, but thanks to some hard work and determination, an original internegative has recently been uncovered, and Massacre are using this preferable element as the source for their 2K restoration. This should easily be the best NIGHTMARE has

ever looked." As of writing, this release has not happened, and perhaps is unlikely in light of the Severin Films release…

SEVERIN FILMS

In June 2023 Severin Films officially announced a forthcoming release of NIGHTMARES with features never before seen in a restored version. In August 2023, this edition appeared in a 4K Ultra HD transfer.

The Severin Films 3-disc set includes many of the extras from the Code Red and 88 Films discs (notably the commentary tracks), as well as new interviews with Romano Scavolini (in Italian with English subtitles), a short but sweet interview with Tom Savini, an interview with the seldom talked about FX artist Robin Stevens (who also shares some photos from her personal collection), a visit to filming locations with *Rue Morgue* writer Michael Gingold, and a nice booklet written by Nathaniel Thompson.

How does our favorite slasher look in 4K Ultra HD? Some scenes have that slick 4K "view master" appearance — those shot in and around Times Square almost look like a live video — but for the most part, I'm happy enough with the Blu-ray transfer that's included on disc 2. I'm thrilled people went to great lengths to deliver this "most complete version ever assembled"*, but let's be honest here, folks: films like NIGHTMARE, LAST HOUSE ON THE LEFT (1972), and a host of the more hardcore slasher classics *benefit* when the quality isn't as shiny as the latest Marvel movie. Not that this 4K scan looks that *pristine*, but a film like NIGHTMARE was never

* As quoted on the Severin Films website and their 2023 4K/Blu-ray sleeve.

intended to be seen on high-def televisions in suburban living rooms. If you're ever lucky enough to attend a 35mm screening or obtain a VHS copy on the Continental Video label, you will surely see what I mean.

Included on disc 3 is DAMAGED: THE VERY BRITISH OBSCENITY OF DAVID HAMILTON GRANT, a feature length documentary centred on the notorious UK film distributor. Created specifically for this package, director Sarah Appleton delivers an extensive look into Grant's background and controversies before he became connected with the distribution of NIGHTMARE. It's a solid film that stands on its own and I believe would've done well had it hit the film festival circuit. There are also four short films produced by Grant for those who simply can't get enough.

A must own for collectors, Severin Films even had a slipcover with original art created just for the occasion (the disc itself comes with a switchable cover featuring both the US and UK poster images).

Although not officially part of the 3-disc set, Severin offered (and may still be offering at the time of this book's publication) a novelization of the film written by Michael Gingold, who horror fans may recognize from his years as editor of both *Fangoria* and *Rue Morgue* magazines, not to mention a series of horror and sci-fi newspaper ad books. The 193-page novel is a fun treat for fans, and features some extra kill scenes, some more interaction between the characters, and best of all a fun twist on the infamous finale.

Knowing Michael was a long-time fan of the film, I invited him to talk with me about his novelization.

INTERVIEW WITH MICHAEL GINGOLD

NICK CATO: Did you get to see NIGHTMARE during its initial run?

MICHAEL GINGOLD: I was a little too young to see NIGHTMARE when it first played theaters, though I was definitely intrigued by the newspaper ads — particularly when they quoted the *Daily News* review calling it "repulsive, offensive, degrading," etc. And I read about the Tom Savini controversy at the time, which also piqued my interest. I didn't wind up seeing it until a couple of years later on VHS, and by that point I was kind of burned out on slasher movies. It definitely struck me as one of the nastier films of that type, and it seemed to confirm all the awful things I had heard about Times Square and 42nd Street at the time, which I didn't experience first-hand until a year or so after that.

How do you think the film has aged?

I hadn't seen NIGHTMARE in many years when I got the gig from Severin to both write the novelization and put together a couple of the extras for the Blu-ray. Looking at it again in those contexts, it confirmed what a couple of the interviewees had said: that Romano Scavolini had changed things as he went along. Characters reference events that we haven't seen happen, and some of the story progression doesn't quite make sense. It also struck me this time just how cynical and nihilistic the movie is: there aren't many positive characters, and the mother, Susan, is a pretty awful person! It definitely catches the ambience of New York City at the time very well, which stands out more when you watch it now since the city has been cleaned up since then.

How did your involvement with the novelization of the film come about?

I've been a fan and collector of novelizations since around 1979—not long before NIGHTMARE started shooting! I had always wanted to write one, and when Severin began putting out books tied in with some of their disc releases, starting with CRUEL JAWS, I asked [Severin co-founder and CEO] David Gregory if he would consider me for one of those. He came back to me with NIGHTMARE, which I thought would be a really fun one to tackle. It turned out to be the biggest and most fun challenge I've ever had as a writer.

Can you tell us about your novelization, without spoiling anything you may have added or removed from the screenplay version?

One of the challenges was that NIGHTMARE isn't very heavy on plot and characterization, but at the same time, that left a lot of room to fill in the blanks and expand on what was there on the screen. Unfortunately, there wasn't a copy of Scavolini's screenplay available for me to work from; none of the people we interviewed for the disc documentary had one. I did receive a few clues about deleted scenes from photos Severin provided, and descriptions of moments that were shot but not used in the final feature that were mentioned in the interviews, or in newspaper articles from the time.

I also added a number of situations that are referenced by the characters but are unseen in the movie, and expanded on things like the government-backed program that George is part of before he escapes. One of the key things was to get into the characters' heads, to further explore their behavior and motivations—and in Susan's case, make her a little less shrill and hysterical and understand her a little better.

One of the interesting things I found when translating NIGHTMARE to the page was that a lot of the gore it's notorious for is contained in the flashbacks to George murdering his parents, and there aren't actually many killings in the main plot. So I added a few new ones, working them in so they made sense within the overall story. I'm especially proud of the death set-piece in the 42nd Street grindhouse, which I think is pretty scary and tragic. Not only that, but it planted the seed for a new epilogue that also pays off on the increased exploration of that government program. Here and in most of the other murder scenes, I wrote them from the victim's point of view, to keep the identification with them and thus make them more frightening.

In general, the idea was to come up with enough character and incident to develop NIGHTMARE's story to novel length, while staying true to what's in the movie.

Was this your first piece of fiction and do you prefer writing fiction or nonfiction?

NIGHTMARE was my first work of longform fiction, and while journalistic writing is still my

first love, this gave me the chance to exercise a different creative muscle, and it was a very satisfying experience. Even though it was based on a prior work, it allowed me to tap into my imagination to come up with all the additional material, and I'm definitely interested in doing more. The experience did give me some respect for how long the process can take, though. I've read interviews where authors have talked about writing a novelization in a week, or even a weekend, and I don't know how they did it!

You also host an extra feature on the Severin release dealing with NIGHTMARE shooting locations. I've heard rumors they shot the final kill sequence in my hometown of Staten Island. Is there any truth to that you're aware of?

In all my research into NIGHTMARE's locations for the Severin featurette, I was never able to figure out where the exteriors seen in the final flashback were shot. I hadn't heard the rumors about them being filmed in Staten Island, and no one connected with the film that I talked to could remember. I assumed that the actual parents' murders were shot somewhere different, like a set in Manhattan, but I was never able to confirm exactly where those took place either!

SEVEN

MORE DAMAGED BRAINS

Guest essays and an interview with 42nd Street Pete

Over the years I've met quite a few fans of NIGHTMARE, many of whom write in the horror community. I asked several if they'd be interested in sharing their thoughts in this book. The following are all new pieces by some of my favorite writers in the horror genre, who happen to be genuine fans of the film as well as accomplished fiction and film commentators. They've each brought in ideas and opinions that I think fans of NIGHTMARE will enjoy.

A NEEDLE IN THE SLASHER HAYSTACK: ROMANO SCAVOLINI'S NIGHTMARES IN A DAMAGED BRAIN

by Jerome Reuter

While watching NIGHTMARES IN A DAMAGED BRAIN for the first time, I wasn't sure what to expect. Aside from being one of the many slasher titles that flooded the market during the 1980s, there was nothing else I knew about it. Because I had grown up during the nineties, I had missed out on the craze from the previous decade. Fortunately, I was able to familiarize myself with 1980s slashers with the advent of home video. Titles such as SLEEPAWAY CAMP, MANIAC COP, AND SILENT NIGHT, DEADLY NIGHT became fixtures of my Friday nights as I was transported into a world of scantily clad bodies and gratuitous killing. When I finally got around to viewing this particular title from Italian director Romano Scavolini, I was pleasantly surprised. It wasn't just a matter of discovering something that had slipped under my radar; it was closer to finding a needle in the proverbial haystack. While many slasher entries I had watched during my adolescence are still enjoyable, there's no denying that a great many of them rely on clichés and tropes that are formulaic and predictable. NIGHTMARE was something unique that went far beyond my expectations.

While the slasher film is synonymous with villains who are over the top in both their appearance and the ambiguous ways in which they dispatch their victims, NIGHTMARE contains a truly unique antagonist in George Tatum. He's the by-product of psychosis, childhood trauma, and is unable to be rehabilitated with experimental medication. From the very beginning, Scavolini literally throws back the veil and establishes the tortured state in which he exists. As Tatum peeks under his bedsheet, he's confronted with his past — the severed head of a victim staring at him, a scene Jörg Buttgereit would pay homage to in SCHRAMM (1993). As a patient of a psychiatric institution, it's made clear early on that Tatum is criminally insane and unfit for life in the outside world; in other words, he's institutionalized. While the reasons for his incarceration and afflictions are lazily delivered via exposition dialogue, there's no denying Scavolini does a wonderful job at depicting the traits of a murderer whose crimes are intertwined with sexuality.

Much like MANIAC, which had been released the previous year, NIGHTMARE manages to briefly capture the underbelly of New York City. The scene of Tatum walking through Times Square with its adult theatres (one of which is advertising Tinto Brass' CALIGULA) and stripshows illustrate the red-light fever of the city in the early 1980s. Not holding back from displaying the degradation of the nightlife, we're treated to a striptease, complete with Tatum's wide-eyed gaze as he becomes immersed in the spectacle. One could make the assumption that this is a triggering moment for him, as it doesn't take long for him to step out of the shadows and strike. It's here where the link between Tatum and the sexuality found in his crimes is firmly established. The only murder depicted onscreen by Tatum as an adult illustrates the sexual pleasure he derives from murder. During a home invasion killing, Tatum slices the throat of a female victim and, using the knife as a phallic extension, slowly plunges it into her chest. On his face he wears an expression that one might see from someone achieving sexual release.

Although sleaze is certainly one of the film's definitive elements in regard to its grittier depictions of sex and violence, there's one aspect that sometimes goes overlooked. Upon closer examination of Tatum, he almost comes

across as being a sympathetic character. As the film progresses, one gets the notion that he has no control over his actions and is himself a victim of his compulsive nature and the inept care of his doctors. Even when he arrives in Florida to stalk his estranged family, he seems to be battling his inner psyche and struggling to regain control of the situation, at one point even calling one of his doctors in a last grasp for help. Throughout the film actor Baird Stafford portrays the character as weak-minded and with the vulnerability of a small child. Through it all, there's a sliver of empathy. Like most serial murderers, he's a repeat offender, yet only some of his crimes are graphically depicted. Other times the film opts to simply show the after effect, forcing the audience to form a mental image. There's a slight glimmer of hope that Tatum can somehow overcome his homicidal nature and rehabilitate himself. Because murder has been so closely linked to his childhood, it's easy to imagine that it's always been a part of him and is firmly embedded in his subconscious. As psychologists will tell you, most adult behavior can easily be traced back to important childhood events.

The aspect of childhood behavior is further explored through Tatum's youngest son, CJ. Coinciding with the storyline involving Tatum's murderous psychosis is that of his estranged family living in Florida. The subplot of his wife trying to raise her children with her new lover is largely uninteresting, and only serves to establish CJ as a character. It's through his childish pranks that the movie continually allows several fake outs to occur which are

effective during a first-time viewing. In one moment the story of "The Boy Who Cried Wolf" is referenced and there's no better description for CJ as a character. While the plotline involving the family can be slow at times, the times when Tatum draws closer to them are tense as the film gradually builds towards its climax. By breaking the plot into a day-by-day basis, the tension mounts with every passing moment. As with some giallo films (and Sergio Leone's defining 1968 western, ONCE UPON A TIME IN THE WEST), Tatum has a recurring flashback that appears multiple times, becoming more complete with each appearance. The final climax is a bloody gun battle and the reveal of Tatum's childhood trauma, plus the insinuation that CJ might follow in his father's blood-drenched footsteps.

While it may never reach the high levels of acclaim that many of its slasher contemporaries have achieved, Scavolini's film is one that stands apart from the herd. For my age group, films like SCREAM (1996) exposed the familiar tropes and took the element of anticipation away from many of the older titles we rented on our Friday nights. NIGHTMARE is the film that I continually turn to as the most underrated slasher title of all time — Scavolini might not have struck gold, but it's a film that certainly carries weight. You won't find any clever one-liners here, just a cold depiction of madness-fueled violence.

NIGHTMARE IN A DAMAGED BRITAIN: A REMINISCENCE

by Gary McMahon

My first exposure to Romano Scavolini's ferocious NIGHTMARES IN A DAMAGED BRAIN was during the infamous 'video nasties' controversy – a period in the early 1980s when a variety of films were banned on video in the UK.

Back then, Britain was a strange place.

The DPP (Director of Public Prosecutions) list of 'video nasties' was first made public in June 1983. The list was modified monthly as prosecutions failed or were dropped. In total, seventy-two films appeared on the list at one time or another. Thirty-nine were successfully prosecuted under the Obscene Publications Act. The remaining thirty-three were not prosecuted or had unsuccessful prosecutions. Ten films from the list are still banned in the UK because they have not yet been resubmitted for classification by any distributors or have been rejected for classification.

I remember I had a regular correspondence with a guy in Derby, or somewhere. His contact details were in a home-printed fanzine to which I subscribed. I would write this guy a letter with a list of the titles I wanted, and he'd send me his latest lists of pirated 'video nasties' and other films that were, for one reason or another, unavailable to legally obtain in Britain. Whenever he sent me videos, he'd always put a home-made trailer reel after the films – a little teaser for the other titles in his collection.

NIGHTMARES IN A DAMAGED BRAIN was somewhere near the middle of my own list of "must-see" films. I'd read a little about it in imported US magazines and some of those shoddy little photocopied fanzines, but my knowledge of the film was limited. All I knew was that it was meant to be strong stuff and a friend of a friend knew someone who had allegedly been arrested for owning a copy (a claim that remains unsubstantiated).

So I sent off my postal order and I waited. A few weeks later, I received a padded envelope containing VHS copies of whatever films I'd ordered – and Scavolini's opus was one of them. I don't recall the others in that specific package, but something tells me that one of them was Pier Paolo Pasolini's SALÒ (1975).

But the titles aren't important. Only the sense of excited anticipation.

What I do remember is sitting in my room with the lights out and the curtains closed – to shut out any ambient light that might affect the poorly-copied images on the small screen of my portable television – and opening a beer.

The quality of the video was terrible. I couldn't hear any of the dialogue. It must have been a third or fourth generation copy. Everything onscreen was drowned in a sea of swirly darkness. I watched the film with no idea what was going on; the plot was lost to me because of the poor sound and picture quality. I couldn't even make out the actors' faces.

I saw brief flashes of what looked like horrendous scenes: a woman's severed head in a pile of viscera on a bed, the eyes and mouth open, as if she were speaking to someone. A vicious attack with an axe. Various bloody stabbings. A close-up of a headless neck spurting a geyser of blood.

There were also scenes with people walking through the grimy 1980s streets of New York, sitting in rooms – sometimes strapped into a chair.

I couldn't follow it at all, but I couldn't switch it off either. There was something about it – a sense of grim meaning beneath the swimming grainy darkness – that held my attention. I knew there was more going on here than just mindless gore, even though I had no idea what it was.

Watching the film was like trying to glean understanding from some time-faded artefact. I think I watched it a further two or three times, each time getting a little more from the images, but still not understanding the story because, to me, there seemed to be no story. And it didn't matter.

I had no idea of the quality of the performances, the direction, or the special effects, because I could barely even see them. This all added to the sleazy allure of the film, the mythical quality it had achieved in my imagination long before I'd even seen it. A quality that persisted in this bastardised form, this strange, static-sodden replica of a film I never thought I'd get to see any other way.

It felt like I was doing something illicit, forbidden, committing an act that could get me arrested and imprisoned for a long time if anyone ever found out. It was exciting. It was dangerous.

It's a feeling I miss.

I AM GEORGE TATUM… WELL, SORTA…

by Andre Duza

It was a week before I was set to go off to boarding school. I was eleven years old. My mom took me to the movies every day as sort of a last chance bonding experience. I was a child heading down a dark path due to a traumatic experience a few years earlier. My single mother's last resort for me was boarding school. It was a confusing time, filled with a mixture of fear and excitement. NIGHTMARE was playing at the Goldman Theater in Philly as the first film of a triple feature that included ALLIGATOR, and some random, Z-level kung fu flick that was more Godfrey Ho/ASSO Asia Films, than Chang Cheh/Shaw Brothers.

ALLIGATOR was the film that we both really wanted to see. Neither of us knew anything about NIGHTMARE, but my mother assumed it was just another run-of-the-mill slasher flick. Not that she condoned my weird obsession with extreme horror, but she figured it was nothing I hadn't seen, and to be quite honest, she has always been a bit of an undercover horror fan herself, even if her taste in films is much more pedestrian, restrained, and preferably devoid of any sexual content. Her ideal films are generally populated by giant, irradiated insects, and things that go bump in the night, and there's always a clear distinction between good and evil.

The theater lights dimmed. The room filled with marijuana smoke as was customary during marathon movie-watching sessions at the Goldman. That was the first sign of my mother's dismay. But it was so commonplace that I think she just ignored it and hoped that I would do the same. Then the movie started.

I remember being both disturbed and fascinated by the film's unrelenting glimpse at George Tatum's descent into madness, and how he seemed to both relish and be repulsed by his own inclinations and actions. I didn't know why at the time, but it was because, in some way, I could relate.

I'd tried not to look as into the film as I actually was whenever my mother would glance over at me. Then, when she'd look away, I'd glance at her, equally fascinated by what was going on in her head as I was by the film. Due to her almost puritanical ideas regarding sexual subject matter, I knew it was eating her up inside. I knew that she was worried about how I was processing all this lurid imagery, and how it would affect me. I thought that, at any second, she was going to drag my ass right out of the theater. But she never did. Instead, she sat there looking extremely tense.

Her reaction in the days that followed was to say nothing about it, as if that would somehow make all the ugliness that she had witnessed at the Goldman go away. But I kept coming at her with questions.

"Why did George kill that lady who was sitting on top of his father, smacking him? And why was she doing that? Why was he talking to that naked lady on the phone, and why did he foam at the mouth because of it? Was she a witch or something?" My mother's response every time was to change the subject.

You see… In a sense, I *was* George Tatum. Although she knew that back then, I didn't fully understand it until I revisited NIGHTMARE as an adult, in the 1990s, when I happened upon the film at a local video store while trying to find something to rent that I hadn't already seen a million times. When I picked up the box and turned it over, the memories all came flooding back to me…

Because of my mom's reaction to the film all those years ago, I had put it out of my mind, and I often wondered if my memory of it wasn't just a figment of my overactive imagination, influenced by my own unsavory childhood experience, the repository of violent scenes from various horror films that stood out to me as somewhat therapeutic, and the murky, unclean aesthetic of parts of downtown Philly in the 1980s, which was very similar to New York as depicted in the film.

While the violent incident at the root of my own neurosis didn't involve parricide, nor was it as rife with bloodletting, there was a sexual component to it, and the emotional impact was similarly life-altering. Like George, I went through years of therapy, and I was plagued with hallucinations of a violent nature. Thankfully there were no severed heads playing peek-a-boo from the foot of my bed, but there were fully realized revenge scenarios, usually perpetrated against male authority figures who I felt had gone too far. George's sickness culminated in murder, while mine culminated in my lashing at several male authority figures; attacking one teacher with a broken hockey stick, another with a meat cleaver, and throwing my grandfather through a window when I was seventeen. My eventual saving grace was more therapy. I guess George wasn't so lucky.

When I finally sat down to rewatch the film as an adult, I was surprised at how, despite possessing some of the typical shortcomings of many of the lower budget exploitation fare of the era, NIGHTMARE was a much deeper, more layered film than it gets credit for, and a real attempt by Romano Scavolini to delve into the mind of a truly sick person. It was then that everything made sense.

Funny how life works sometimes.

A DAMAGED BRAIN IS NOT UNLIKE MASTURBATING

by Philip LoPresti

I first saw DAMAGED BRAIN when I was fourteen or fifteen. I equate this first viewing to seeing a naked woman for the first time — which at that point I had yet to experience first-hand, as that would happen a year later — or discovering masturbation, which I had regularly been doing for at least three years by the time my friend arrived at my house with a VHS copy he'd scored from a bootleg catalogue. The ad inside claimed it was in its uncut glory. We sat in my room that night smoking stolen cigarettes and watched the carnage unfold. Two moths drawn into a flame from which we would reemerge chain-smoking men. We came, we saw, and we were wiser because of it. My eyes were open. That's what my fourteen-year-old self thought, anyway, because when you're fourteen you think stupid shit like that.

Now, by that time, I had already been raised on a steady diet of horror films. I had seen raw classics such as THE LAST HOUSE ON THE LEFT (1972) and THE TEXAS CHAIN SAW MASSACRE (1974) and frequently watched off the wall films like DEMONS and RE-ANIMATOR (1985), but I don't believe I'd seen a film that was just straight up mean. It was nasty and nihilistic in its approach and that was new to me. No one iin our circle had seen it, nor seen anything like it. We were passing through a gateway into a whole new corner of horror, the sleaze-filled kind. It led to such discoveries as MANIAC (1980), MOTHER'S DAY (1980) and PIECES (1982), to name just a few.

The film itself feels as off-kilter as the unbalanced mental patient as its core. Some scenes are genuinely effective because of the use of camera work and editing, followed suddenly by scenes that feel haphazard. It may be a mood killer for some, but for me it only adds to the overall feel. The gore is plentiful, and the acting is all over the place, ranging from way underplayed to completely over the top, which again, adds to the insanity of the entire piece. There are very few things like NIGHTMARES, before or since.

Watching it now, all these years later, it still retains its bite. But I can also laugh at it, something I don't think I did on my first few viewings as a kid. I didn't see the ridiculousness through the gore and nastiness. Sure, it's still mean-spirited, but it is also so off the wall in its delivery that as an adult I can't take it too seriously. And it shouldn't be taken too seriously. The film revels in its own filth, but that's what I love most about it. That's what I love about a lot of films from what I consider the heyday of horror. Never shy away. Just when you think you've gone far enough, go a little further and do it with the giddiness of a child that has yet to experience the actual horrors of life.

AN INTERVIEW WITH 42ND STREET PETE

As publisher of the long running magazine, *Grindhouse Purgatory*, and the recent *Grindhouse Resurrection*, Pete Chiarella (aka 42nd Street Pete) grew up in New York's Times Square and seedy theaters in New

Jersey, and through his work with Something Weird Video has done much to preserve countless grindhouse films. He has also been involved with New Jersey's largest horror convention, Chiller Theatre, since its inception. I've been an admirer of Pete's work for quite a while, and was eager to ask him about NIGHTMARE, a film that, like myself, he saw on a double bill with MOTHER'S DAY.

NICK CATO: Before NIGHTMARE, were you familiar with Romano Scavolini? There are those who say he worked in hardcore sex films, but I only know he was cinematographer on some softcore dramas and comedies.

42ND STREET PETE: I wasn't, but if he did direct hardcore, he'd probably have used a pseudonym. That's what most of those guys did.

NIGHTMARE was released in 1981, but I didn't see it until 1983 when it was double billed with MOTHER'S DAY. I understand you attended that double bill as well?

You know, I thought it was double billed in '81? I'm pretty sure I saw it when it first came out. On 42nd Street, they always double-billed films even when they were new. They would double bill in Jersey, too, but by the mid-80s they weren't.

But I can tell you who I was with at the

screening: Kevin from Chiller Theatre, this punk rocker named Fred, and this guy who used to be the roadie for the Sic Fucks, Mark. So, we're in Fred's Ford Fairlane, and we decided to go see this double feature up at Cinema 46, in Totawa, New Jersey. It was a twin theater, and the thing about it is they were the only place in Jersey that showed things like DAWN OF THE DEAD (the unrated one), DAY OF THE DEAD, and CHAINSAW 2. I think this screening of NIGHTMARE was unrated if I remember right.

So we went in, and they have the poster in the lobby, it had that blank space where Tom Savini's name was taped over due to some kind of legal thing.

Kevin and Fred didn't *indulge*, but me and Mark did. We had a plethora of alcoholic beverages and weed with us. So, we're in the middle of these films, and they're running, and y'know, in NIGHTMARE I dug the whole 42nd Street deal, all that footage?

Right.

And the weird part was, after the movie, guess where we wound up? Show World! [The porn emporium near Port Authority Bus Terminal on 42nd Street, where early scenes in NIGHTMARE were filmed.]

Anyway, we're watching this whole thing, and we're drinking and smoking, and we were the *only people in the fucking theater*! So, y'know, we're getting rowdy, beer bottles are rolling down to the front. So then we lighten up, we're laughing at certain scenes … where we really lost it was at the decapitation, because it was an obvious mannequin, and it was shooting blood all over the place.

So, NIGHTMARE was first, MOTHER'S DAY was second, and we were pretty rowdy, then all of a sudden the second movie ends, and as I turn around there's two cops standing by the exit. And I'm like, "Why the fuck did they call the cops when they could've just told us to calm down?" So I said to the guys, "Let's be cool and just get out of here," so we slithered by the cops, getting dirty looks from them. Then we get in Fred's Ford Fairlane, and we take off … and his brake pedal goes right through the fucking floor!

Somehow we get back to where my truck is, and we decide we're going to go to New York and go to Show World, because we're stimulated by the fact they showed Show World in NIGHTMARE. So, we went cruising around New York, picking fights with hookers and shit like that before we got to the place.

Having recently watched the DVD, I'm thinking Scavolini had to somehow be connected to the porn industry, just being able to film scenes inside Show World. And when they shot that scene of the killer walking down 42nd Street, passed the Liberty Theater, and you knew that was Blackjack Books, but for some reason they never filmed above a certain height. Maybe not to advertise those places? Maybe they were worried about getting sued? Who knows?

In an interview with [actor] Baird Stafford on the Code Red DVD, he said those scenes of him strutting through Times Square were total guerilla filmmaking. No permits, nothing. Just a guy with a camera following him in a car.

Yeah, sort of like an Andy Milligan deal. It's kind of like when Chris Rock was going to shoot in my section at Liquidators, a video store I worked at. They sent me home. They had gone around to all of these stores that were run by the mob, and most of them were like "There's no fucking way we're gonna let you shoot in here!"

This is why I think Scavolini might have been directing porn at one point, but it had to be under a different name. I mean, Milligan shot porn that we're obviously never gonna see. But I don't know why some critics blasted NIGHTMARE for looking like a porn ... why is that a bad thing? You wanted these grindhouse films to look gritty and real. They shot this thing in 1979, 1980. Scavolini might've been one of the last guys doing that guerilla filmmaking thing.

So, the double bill you attended at Cinema 46 was really empty?

Yeah! I think this must've been in the middle of the week. When I was growing up, new films were released on Wednesdays. But toward that era, it would've been Friday. So I'm guessing we maybe rolled in on a Monday or Tuesday. At the time I was living with someone, and she wasn't into these films. So it was probably a Tuesday, when we usually had our boy's night-out thing. I had made the mistake of taking her to see HUMANOIDS FROM THE DEEP and she said, "Never again." [Laughs]

Can you tell us about the NIGHTMARE film canister you were in possession of? There have been rumors of a never-before-seen shot of CJ's young friend Tony hanging from a noose. A picture even surfaced a couple years ago online.

Mike [Vraney] from Something Weird Video had a ton of shit for sale on eBay. Some of the things I bought even said Something Weird on the reels, so they must've dumped a bunch of stuff somewhere. I think one was HUNCHBACK OF THE MORGUE (1973), and the other one said NIGHTMARE on it. I bought both, I figured maybe I could flip these to Code Red, because they were gonna release NIGHTMARE on DVD. I got a hold of [someone at Code Red through Facebook], I told him I had won a NIGHTMARE canister on eBay, and figured I'd let him make me an offer. But he pretty much just said, "Oh, that's nice."

I ended up selling it to [film collector and dealer] Eddie McCale down in South Jersey. Whatever happened to it, I don't know. How many people have 35mm projectors that they can watch this shit on? So, if any company is about to put out another Blu-ray, if they say they have some new footage, maybe they got it from this reel? Who knows. It's just weird how much of this stuff floats around and no one ever gets to see it.

EIGHT

HATED BY CRITICS

Possibly the best known review of NIGHTMARE was written by *New York Times* critic Janet Maslin. For years it was one of the only things related to the film that could be found online, until a barrage of horror film blogs began to show their love (or hate).

Published on the day of the film's U.S. release, Maslin's review, for copyright reasons, cannot be presented here in its three-paragraph entirety. However, you can easily find it online.

While an accomplished and respected film and book critic, Maslin is *not* a horror fan, so her negative review wasn't surprising (and I read it before seeing the film). I'm convinced Maslin attended the film but either left early or brought a book along to read. Despite many attempts over many years to contact her through her social media accounts and emails, I failed to reach her for comment regarding the review. So, in a spirit of fun, let's address a few of her points:

"'NIGHTMARE' is the perfunctory work of Romano Scavolini, a writer-director whose best idea here is to repeat the same gory flashback footage over and over again."

The flashback footage is quite disturbing. Perhaps the goriness of them caused Maslin's attention to get stuck with the visuals and stay away from the mindset of George Tatum, something that is easy to fall into with only one viewing. This statement so early in the review may have excited some of us gorehounds, but I could see it easily turning off horror fans who don't care for the gruesome stuff. And of course, it is an unfair statement on the talent of Scavolini, who has directed over twenty-five films in multiple genres.

"This causes George to dream that there are pieces of people in his bed and to spend his waking hours killing blondes."

This statement made me doubt Maslin stayed for the film's entire running time. In fact, the first woman George kills is a brunette, so perhaps she left the theater earlier than I originally thought. While I always enjoy re-reading this brief review, this comment is a dead giveaway the film wasn't given a fair shot.

"The movie's attempts to present George not just as a standard goon but also as an interesting case study are laughable in the extreme."

I believe comments I made in this book's introduction dispel this opinion. George is one of the more complex characters in slasher film history, even if it isn't easy to see that upon a single viewing or without contemplating the film for more than its gore sequences.

"Mr. Scavolini ... also favors the trick whereby an ostensible scare turns out to be a practical joke. There are about six different variants of this in 'NIGHTMARE.'

No argument there. The "Fake Scare" thing is one of NIGHTMARE's biggest criticisms and she picked up on it right away. They all happen within the first half of the film, so perhaps Maslin *did stay* for at least that long.

As weird as it sounds, I'm a *fan* of Janet Maslin's review. And as Kathleen Ferguson says in her interview, the cast and crew had a copy of it hanging up in their post-production office! I've read her three-paragraph piece countless times since the day it was first published. I love knowing a critic as famous as Maslin even entertained the idea of reviewing this film, although I'm sure it was an assignment and not because she was genuinely curious.

A second negative review was published upon the film's 1981 release in New York's *Daily News*. Like Janet Maslin, critic Bill Carlton's review was just three paragraphs and rated NIGHTMARE zero stars. However, the first sentence of the review went on to be used in promotional ads and eventually, a NIGHTMARE T-shirt design. The quote is:

"This is the most repulsive, offensive, degrading, gory, depraved and horrifying movie ever made."

So, yes, Carlton unintentionally sold the film

to a legion of gorehounds and had most of us salivating with anticipation. The second paragraph of his review describes some of the violence, and adds that one scene featured "guts spilled," so, like Maslin, I wonder if he stayed for the film's complete running time, as there are no scenes of guts being spilled.

When first released, NIGHTMARE was screened at the Embassy II Theater in Times Square, 24 hours a day for a full week. Carlton ends his brief review by stating:

"I suggest police raid the joint about 6 a.m. and they'll net every homicidal maniac in town. Who else would be there?"

In the early 1980s, I think a lot of critics attempted to steer people away from certain "splatter films" by these super-negative reviews. But as would happen with the PMRC and record label warnings a few years later, these reviews only created more anticipation among fans of the genre.

'A PIECE OF JUNK'

"Hate to say it, but "NIGHTMARES IN A DAMAGED BRAIN" (a.k.a. "NIGHTMARE") is a powerfully boring psychological serial killer movie...

"A deranged psychopath is declared harmless after serving as a guinea pig for a new drug that is supposed to have balanced him out. Not so. He heads to Florida and begins terrifying the family now living in the home where he murdered his father and his father's S&M partner with an axe as a kid. His schizophrenia sparks old murderous tendencies and there's a few random murders thrown in (including that of a child).

"This seems to be a pretty favorable entry in the low budget serial killer sub-genre that has been compared to such big dogs as MANIAC and HENRY: PORTRAIT OF A SERIAL KILLER. I couldn't agree less. If only the killer here wasn't such an intermittent character and actually displayed a little more tenacity before getting his ass handed to him by a nine-year-old kid in the 'climactic' conclusion, I may have been able to get 'into' this a little more. The highlight scene, of course, involves a double axe murder which is quite gruesome and splattery. Overall, NIGHTMARE IN A DAMAGED BRAIN is a very forgettable flick."

—The Spastic Cannibal, Buried.com:

"Its flaws are apparent almost immediately. The cast are forgettable and barely competent. The story is stretched thinly and for huge portions of the movie it's really boring. It's very standard slasher stuff and its big reveal at the end is in no way worth the wait.

"No, the only reason NIGHTMARE hasn't been consigned to the bin is purely because of the video nasty tag. What an idiotic event that was, making these nothing movies into sought after collector items.

"The government is saying this movie is too depraved for anyone to see? Who isn't going to want to see it now!?"

—gbhbl.com (Games, Brains & A Head-Banging Life)

"The acting is unsurprisingly nothing of note, although it must be said Stafford's hysteria is something to behold.

'Nightmare' is a nightmare

0 ★

Baird Stafford, Sharon Smith. Directed by Romano Scavolini. Embassy II and other theaters. Running time: 97 minutes. No rating.

THIS IS THE most repulsive, offensive, degrading, gory, depraved and horrifying movie ever made. With violence so graphic—axes between the eyes, heads lopped off, throats slashed and guts spilled—the viewer himself wants to take an ax to the screen.

The plot, for those who require logic, concerns a poor, misunderstood psycho who had a traumatic experience as a child. The shrinks medicate him to no avail. He escapes the nuthouse and goes on a savage murder spree. And since all the cliches in the genre have been bled white—the baby sitter alone, the shower scene, the late-night phone calls—the film relies on psychological twists to create tension. None of it works.

It's being shown at the Embassy II 24 hours a day. I suggest the police raid the joint about 6 a.m. and they'll net every homocidal maniac in town. Who else would be there? —Bill Carlton

"Scavolini's direction is sluggish, with long stretches of the film passing by at a snail's pace.

"There is also a hefty amount of nudity, mainly of the female variety of course, which also proves a bit tiresome after a while.

"Virtually impossible to recommend, NIGHTMARES IN A DAMAGED BRAIN has little going for it other than the effects – so only go near this if you need an 80s gore fix."

—Simon Fitzjohn, movieramblings.com

The final negative review was written by Alan Jones after he attended a UK press screening in 1982. It was published in the 48th issue of STARBURST magazine, and the full review can be found online. Presented here are the highlights:

"This is a piece of junk no matter how you look at it. Director Romano Scavolini betrays his hardcore porn past by adding pointless nudity and plenty of padding to fill up the weak plot and running time. Even horror fans want some semblance of a plot in-between the gore. Speaking of which, the gore scenes here aren't very convincing: the props are too fake and the blood too red and the film is weighed down with a tedious, repetitive flashback. Scavolini's feeble plot will be deciphered early on by anyone with the slightest bit of intelligence.

"There was an air of secrecy around this screening, and vomit bags were handed out, proving that at least showmanship still exists in the industry. Too bad it had to be wasted on such worthless trash. There's no one to blame but yourself if you go to see NIGHTMARE."

Perhaps Maslin and Carlton's reviews are kind compared to Jones'? Either way, even as a fan of NIGHTMARE I've enjoyed its criticisms over the years and felt they had a place in this book. Several critics have felt the film features too much nudity, when in fact it barely has any.

I've yet to meet anyone who thinks the film is just okay. Most either love it or hate it.

NINE

INCARCERATION

David Hamilton Grant takes a hit for the team

By Mike Hunchback

NIGHTMARE was banned in the UK during the 'video nasties' era (see Gary McMahon's essay in chapter seven). Here is a brief history of how this came to be. In the early 1980s, David Hamilton Grant formed a video distribution company, World of Video 2000, and released Scavolini's film in the UK under the title NIGHTMARES IN A DAMAGED BRAIN.

Grant was the UK's self-proclaimed "King of Sexploitation." The staid and draconian obscenity laws in England had created an interesting underworld of smut, everything from under-the-counter photographs and films that gentlemen could purchase on request, to the sort of anti-establishment antics that Grant would cut his teeth on. Britain in the 1970s did not permit the sale or public showing of hardcore pornography, although it was not an offense to own such material. However, several enterprising individuals began to exhibit hardcore films in the private clubs they owned, collecting a handsome sum in membership fees while thumbing their nose at what they perceived an inappropriate involvement of the law in people's personal lives. Grant was one such individual. It is this sense of mischief-at-duty that seems to have really captivated Grant.

From the late 1960s through to the 1970s, Grant produced all kinds of adult content. Some of his films were even short pornographic cartoons, bawdy retellings of fairy tales, such as SINDERELLA (1972) and SNOW WHITE AND THE SEVEN PERVERTS (1973). In an interview with *Punch* magazine in 1978, Grant recalled having "tried for the job of illustrating a book called Love Variations," but when this project failed he decided to turn the images into a film. Grant directed a film version of LOVE VARIATIONS in 1970 under an alias. The film was effectively a sex manual, featuring a couple demonstrating different sexual positions, much like the "white coater" trend in America. It made enough money for Grant to continue his film ventures, but his insistence on hammering away at the moral upper crust of his country was becoming an obsession. Eventually he announced a never-made film called THE SEX LIFE OF JESUS that was to feature both heterosexual and homosexual acts ... perhaps the announcement was just to piss off the Archbishop and his high-profile nemesis Mary Whitehouse.

Along with another sexploitation icon, Ray Selfe, Grant formed Oppidan Pictures, distributing both local and imported softcore films. He also shot many of his own softcore films, almost all of them rip offs of popular UK sex comedies and would shoot extra hardcore scenes for foreign versions.

It's easy to see David Grant was a man who did what he wanted, and one might guess he would have heartily agreed with the notion that "all press is good press". The cross-section of ribald gentlemanly fun and the marketability of scandal is a place Grant seemed most comfortable. One story goes that while working as press on the Peter Sellers film THE MAGIC CHRISTIAN (1969), Grant purposefully invited the media to the set on the same day a scene that required 100 topless models was being shot. Needless to say, the film was widely covered in the press and Grant would continue to toy with scandal when World of Video 2000 came to be. NIGHTMARES IN A DAMAGED BRAIN had been released theatrically with cuts. When Grant distributed the film on video it was the uncut version and without BBFC classification, exploiting the loophole that existed in the early days of British video, Furthermore, like many exploitation film distributors before him, Grant set up a wild publicity stunt to promote the film: outside of a hospital, people were challenged to "Guess the weight of the Damaged Brain," and I'll assume fliers for the film were handed out along with it. Where Grant got the brain from (or if it was even real) is anyone's guess, but suffice it to say it helped bring attention to the film and eventually landed Grant and a few of his partners in prison. On February 3, 1984, Grant was sentenced to eighteen months, but I've read he served twelve, and in another article, six. Grant was found guilty under Section Two of the Obscene Publications Act

Consequently NIGHTMARE became one of the most sought after of the 'video nasties', but the notoriety didn't pan out as Grant might have hoped and World of Video 2000 was soon liquidated. Grant continued to make news when it was suspected he had produced child pornography in the 1960s and 1970s. Pictures of Grant surfaced with Peter

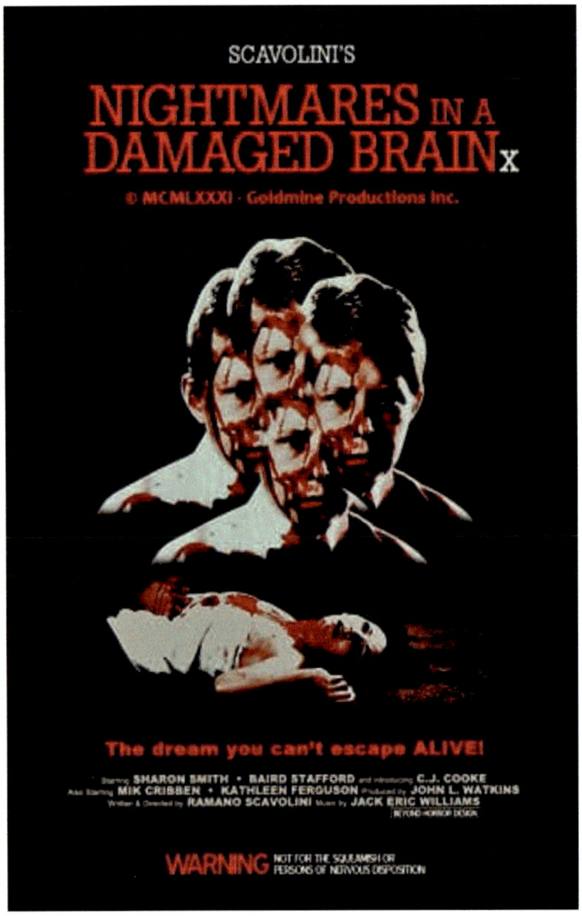

Glencross, a business manager for a travel guide that turned out to be a front for pedophiles. The fervor that surrounds any reference to pedophilia is understandably intense. But one detail that often gets overlooked when discussing Grant in light of these allegations concerns NIGHTMARES IN A DAMAGED BRAIN and the fact that some factions of the press have disingenuously described it as a film that features children in sex scenes. NIGHTMARES IN A DAMAGED BRAIN, as we know, follows the plight of George Tatum after witnessing as a boy his father having sex. To anyone who has seen the film, the idea that this scene should be considered "an obscene article featuring a child in a sex scene" is frankly ridiculous. However, the number of people who have seen the film is but a small fraction compared to the majority the news media cares about. Grant's 1984 arrest and imprisonment was for a so-called 'video nasty' at a time when 'video nasties' were frightening all the wrong people; the film didn't simply lack BBFC classification but appeared to flaunt doing so, making the video uncut when the BBFC had only recently classified a cut theatrical version. I have zero opinion on Grant beyond the history and the known facts. Whatever kind of person he may have been, it's still wrong and unforgivable to sink to the low of spinning the facts of the case so profoundly for a salacious headline.

But the mystery only thickens. Perhaps fed up with his stuffy home in England, Grant moved to Turkey after his release from prison and … opened a deli? But, according to regional British newspaper, the *Slough, Eron & Windsor Observer*, Grant had been kicked out of Turkish Cyprus after a drug racket and child pornography ring was exposed. He left there in 1988 with a supposed nasty reputation of assault and dealing drugs which "corrupted thousands of children." Researching Grant's days in Turkey is difficult. There seem to be two camps of thought, one that Grant was consistently involved in child sex slave rings and child pornography, and one that he was the victim of conspiracy, his political enemies possibly teaming up with one of Grant's personal enemies, Clive Godden, the husband of a woman who ultimately left him for Grant. One Turkish news article details a shovel attack between the two men. Even on the blogs, the fury flies: the comments section of one (needleblog. wordpress.com) devolves into an insane battle in which someone claiming to be Clive Godden himself starts firing off furious quips. Could it be that a crossed lover decided to destroy Grant's

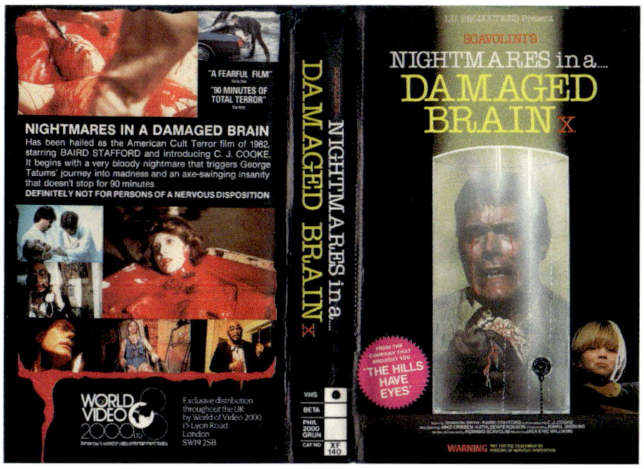

life? Because of the overwhelming conflicting details, it's impossible to say. Grant died in 1991, but as if the story couldn't get any weirder, some of the blogs hint that he faked his own death or outright claim to know Grant is alive, having talked to him in person, and that he is simply lining up the true facts before he emerges to clear his name for good.

As of this writing, the last few years have kicked up an amazing storm of old dirt surrounding Grant's alleged involvement in one of his most gruesome accusations, being an orchestrator of the Elm Guest House child prostitution ring. As the story was originally reported in the British press, the Elm Guest House was a lodging where an underground society of pedophiles could go to commit sex crimes on underage boys, with some perpetrators said to be leading government officials and highest-ranking MI5 and MI6 officers. It was the kind of fodder that the press loves to repeat.

In an edition of PANORAMA broadcast on October 6th, 2015, a former Elm Guest House prostitute was interviewed who claimed that he was unaware of any MPs visiting the brothel.

On one hand, it appears to be the McMartin's Day Care trial or CAPTURING THE FRIEDMANS all over again, a case of mass hysteria, fired by the press, becomes the tool of those who want to bury personal, political or social enemies. On the other hand, it's hard to reconcile all of these mysterious loose ends that indeed rise to the surface when looking at Grant's (supposed) final years.

In an almost mind-bendingly perverse twist, the outcome of this decades long faked-death-or-not/child pornography/pedophile ring is not really the headline. In the unlikely event that satisfactory truths ever surface concerning David Hamilton Grant, they wouldn't be more interesting than the endlessly convoluted story that this chapter merely hints at. The twist is that the public's willingness to be a smear-campaign hungry mob is in fact born from the same base recesses of our psyche that are at the heart of our fascination with indecent sex and violence, the same territory David Hamilton Grant gleefully exploited in the films he produced and distributed.

Damaged brains indeed.*

---

* Sources:
https://www.google.com/amp/s/theneedleblog.wordpress.com/2015/04/12/elm-guest-house-and-why-the-truth-mattersi/amp/
https://scepticpeg.wordpress.com/2017/10/18/elm-guest-house-carole-kasir-inquest/
https://www.independent.co.uk/news/uk/crime/abuse-victims-trafficked-abroad-8478607.html
http://aangirfan.blogspot.com/2013/02/elm-guest-house-david-hamilton-grant.html
https://www.telegraph.co.uk/news/uknews/crime/11877289/Questions-mount-over-troubled-key-witness-in-VIP-abuse-murder-inquiry.html

TEN

COLLECTOR OF NIGHTMARES

The Amazing Collection of Marc Leppla

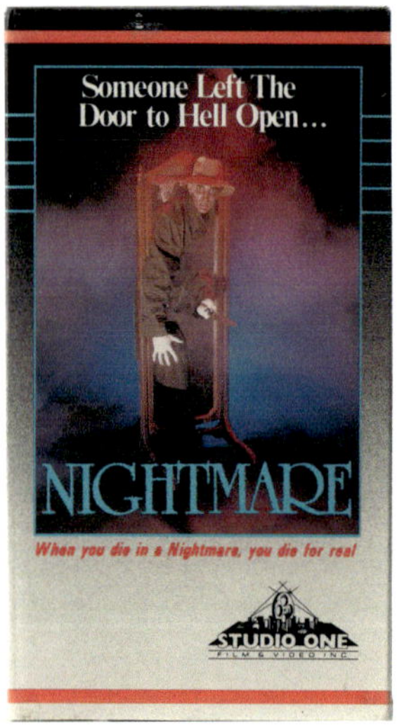

Canada

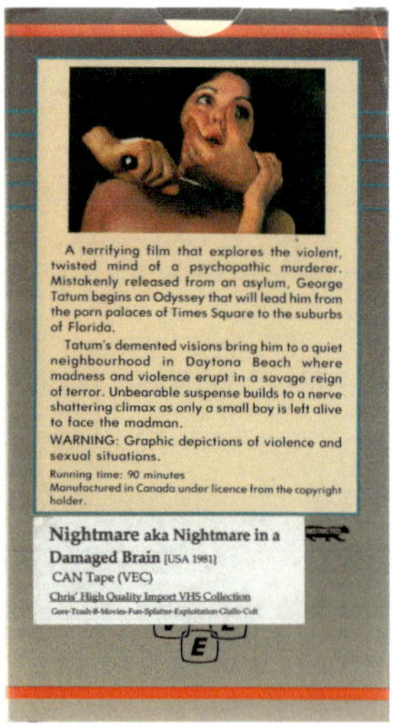

Canada

COLLECTOR OF NIGHTMARES

Among the many NIGHTMARE fans I've met over the years, no one has accumulated a collection as massive as Marc Leppla. He has agreed to share much of his collection for this book, and for that I'm eternally grateful. Feast your eyes, and take note of the alternative titles from around the globe…

France

France

Spain

South Korea

Spain

Mexico

USA

USA

Germany

Germany

Germany

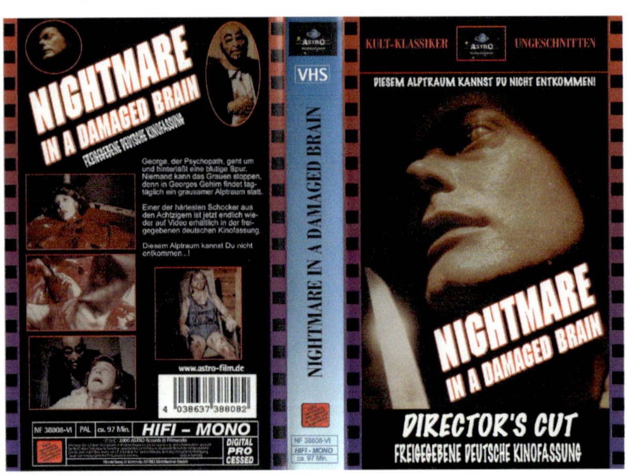

Australia

USA

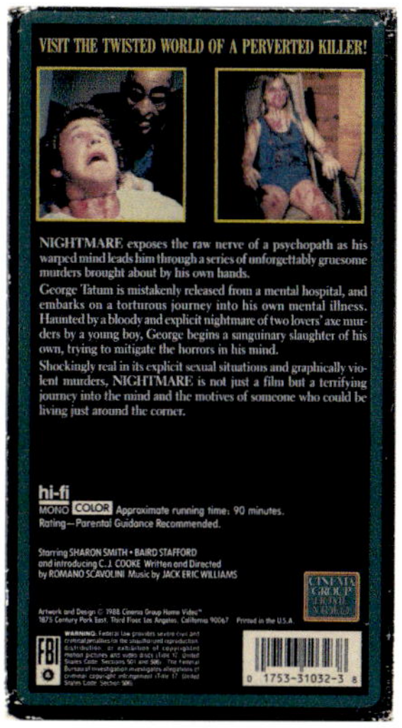

USA

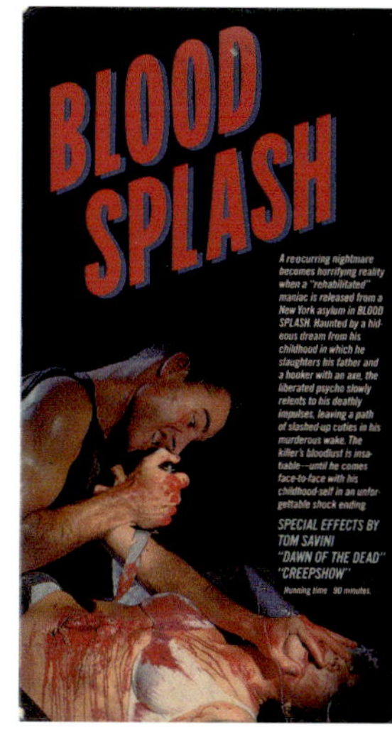

Austria

Austria

Sweden & Finland

Sweden

Japan

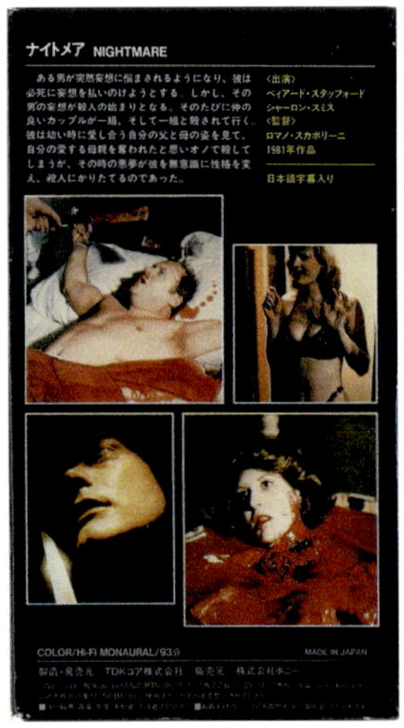

Argentina

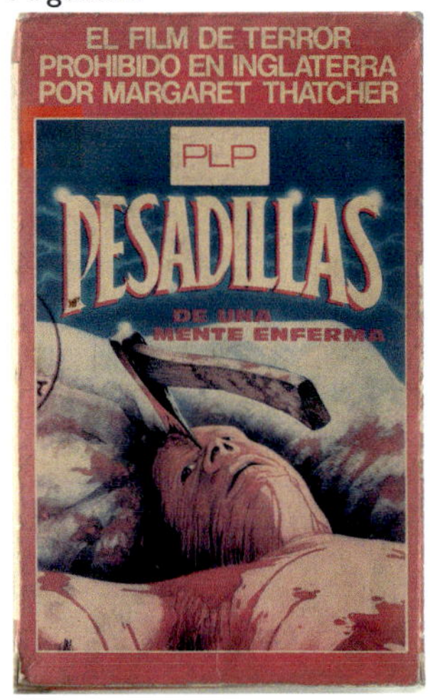

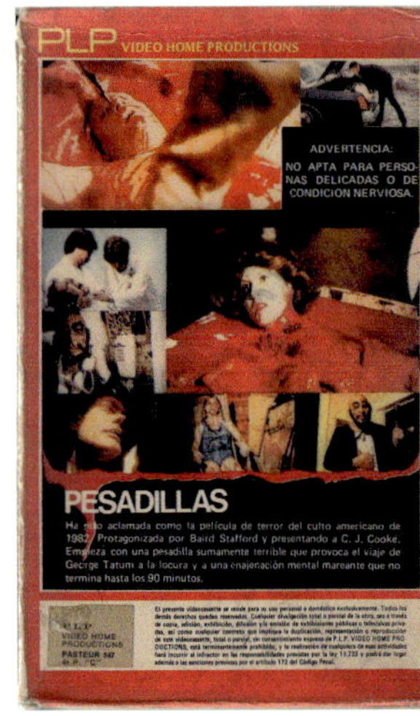

Japan

Argentina

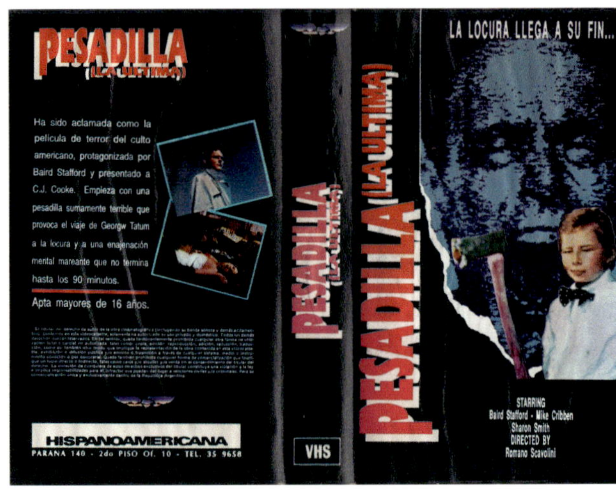

Argentina

Argentina

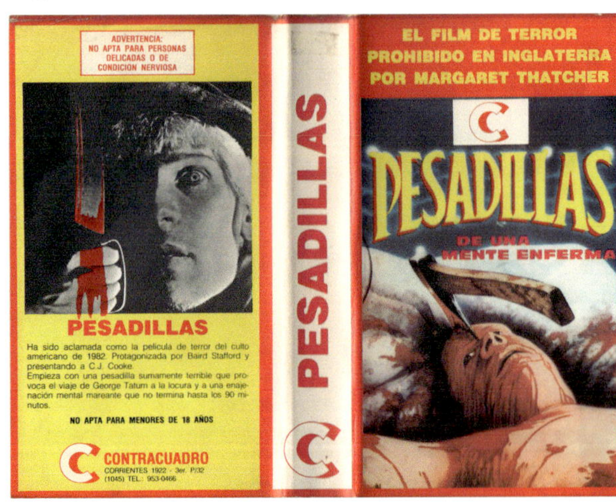

NIGHTMARE press book front.

NIGHTMARE press book interior.

NIGHTMARE press book interior.

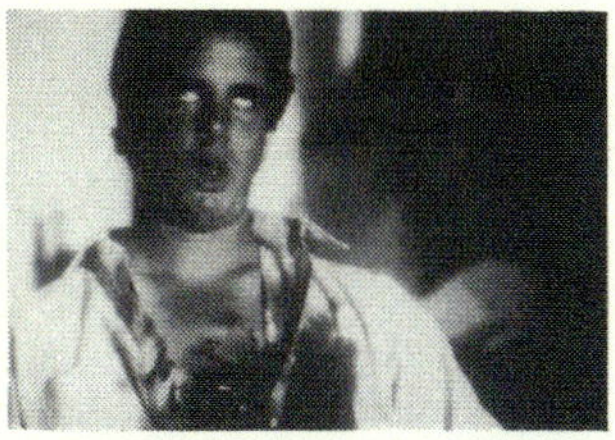

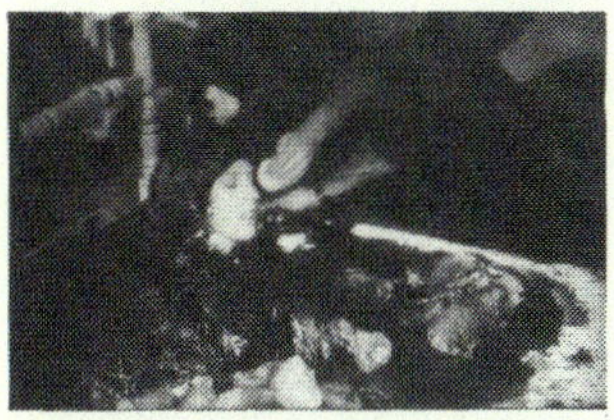

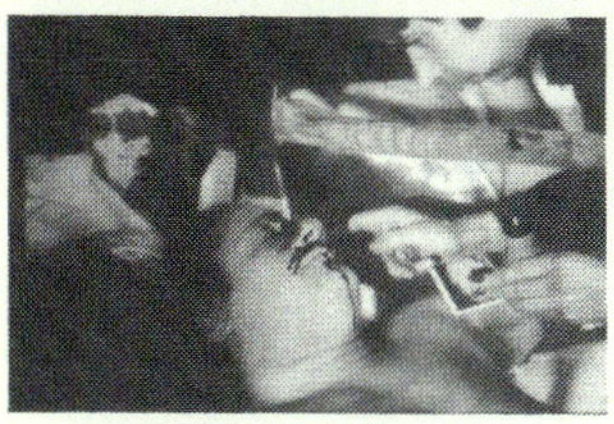

Who Stars in NIGHTMARE?

Who starred in FRIDAY THE 13TH? How about TEXAS CHAINSAW MASSACRE? DAWN OF THE DEAD?

Stumped? It's no surprise –although these were all very successful movies, they didn't rely on the names of performers to sell tickets. The stars of these and many other recently successful movies were not people. The stars were Special Effects.

What is a Special Effect? It can range from Linda Blair's spinning head in THE EXORCIST to the graphically gruesome decapitation in NIGHTMARE, which opens ________ at ________. The Effect can be created by careful editing (Janet Leigh's shower-death in PSYCHO), or by using dummies or machines. NIGHTMARE uses the most sophisticated techniques in its gory imagery, continuing in the tradition of recent, very successful thrillers like DAWN OF THE DEAD and FRIDAY THE 13TH. NIGHTMARE is a bizarre horror epic, spilling blood from New York to Florida. Hearts pound and sweat pours as the suspense builds, inventing new and ever more gruesome methods of doing away with its victims.

Of course, an Effect in itself is only a trick. Whether or not the trick works is dependent largely upon how well it is employed. More often than not, it is the patter and diversion that make a magician's tricks work, and much the same is true in a film. In NIGHTMARE, director-writer ROMANO SCAVOLINI has carefully paced the action, to heighten the effectiveness of each of his 'surprises.' Working carefully with Director of Photography GIANNI FIORE, SCAVOLINI manages to take us into a deranged mind excursion, to let us see what it is like to lose one's mind. And he accomplishes this without ever overlooking his primary purpose: to entertain.

NIGHTMARE stars (in addition to its very SPECIAL Effects) BAIRD STAFFORD, SHARON SMITH and C.J. COOKE. The film has a hauntingly composed original score created by JACK ERIC WILLIAMS.

Taken in combination, the Effects, the direction and writing, and the acting add up to a new recipe for those horror buffs who have been looking for a film to keep them awake. As stated in the film, "It's only a dream, and dreams can't hurt you."

21ST CENTURY DISTRIBUTION CORP.

RUNNING TIME: 97 MINUTES

1650 BROADWAY, NEW YORK, N.Y. 10019
Phone:(212) 541-4722

ACCESSORIES AVAILABLE FROM:
UTA
UNITED THEATRICAL AMUSEMENT
1658 CORDOVA ST., LOS ANGELES, CAL. 90007
TOLL FREE: 800•421-1043 OR (213) 734-0510

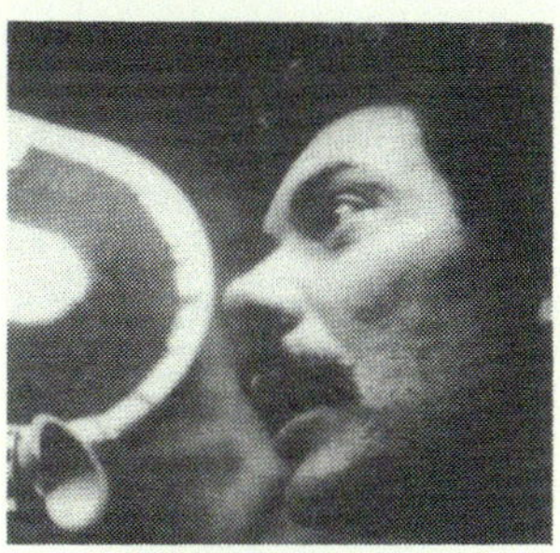

ROMANO SCAVOLINI
Writer-Director

The man responsible for the unique 'feel' of NIGHTMARE is a newcomer to American films, but very well known in Europe. Romano Scavolini's credits include the features THE DEVASTATED, BLIND MAN'S BLUFF (which he wrote and directed), STATE OF SIEGE (starring Joan Collins), THEN, THE LONG MARCH (for Italian television) and A WHITE DRESS FOR MARIALE.

As Director of Photography, Scavolini is even better known, his films including FELLINI (directed by Gideon Bachman), HIS DAY OF GLORY (directed by Edoardo Bruno and a winner at the Berlin Film Festival) and THE NAIVE (directed by G. Baldanello).

JACK ERIC WILLIAMS
Composer

Jack Eric Williams could just as easily be receiving a credit in NIGHTMARE as a performer, since he has achieved considerable recognition for his acting and singing abilities as well as for his composing. Most recently he appeared on Broadway in the Stephen Sondheim / Harold Prince production, SWEENEY TODD. Creating a part that was written with his unique vocal abilities in mind, Williams devasted audiences night after night with his chilling portrayal of the evil Beadle Bamford. His reviews were unanimous raves.

As a composer he has received numerous commissions in the United States and Europe as well as many awards for his versatile and creative writings.

GIANNI FIORE
Director of Photography

Gianni Fiore is considered one of the very best camera operators in the world. He is the first camera operator for almost all of Director of Photography Giuseppe Rotunno's films. As Camera Operator, his films include Visconti's DEATH IN VENICE; Peter Bogdanovich's DAISY MILLER; Fellini's CASANOVA, ORCHESTRA REHEARSAL and THE CITY OF WOMEN; Lina Wertmuller's A NIGHT FULL OF RAIN, Robert Altman's POPEYE; and Francesco Rosi's ONCE UPON A TIME, THE MATTEI FILE, LUCKY LUCIANO and MAN VS. MAN, as well as numerous films which are less well known in the United States.

He brings an unmatched quality and style to the production of NIGHTMARE.

NIGHTMARE press book interior.

NIGHTMARE

CAST

George Tatum	BAIRD STAFFORD
Susan Temper	SHARON SMITH
C.J. Temper	C.J. COOKE
Bob Rosen	MIK CRIBBEN
Barbara	KATHLEEN FERGUSON
Kathy the Babysitter	DANNY RONAN

CREDITS

Director of Photography	GIANNI FIORE
Editor	ROBERT T. MEGGINSON
Music	JACK ERIC WILLIAMS
Production Supervisor	SIMON NUCHTERN
Producer	JOHN L. WATKINS
Executive Producer	DAVID JONES
Written & Directed by	ROMANO SCAVOLINI

SYNOPSIS

NIGHTMARE is a terrifying trip into the mind of a man who is going mad -- and trying desperately to stop himself. It begins with the very nightmare that is the source of all of the terror that is to follow: A man named George is suffering through a graphic dream that depicts the axe murders of a love-making couple.

We cut to a scene in Florida where a much abused babysitter has her hands full trying to control three children in her charge. It is late at night and the kids won't sleep. The kids complain that they've heard a prowler outside. When the babysitter goes to investigate, she is attacked by an unknown person. The police come to investigate, but they can find nothing. We see the youngest child, a troublemaker if there ever was one, as he sits on the steps laughing.

We flash to the nightmare sequence again for another look at the horrifying murder of the couple. When we return to the waking world, we see a doctor talking with George about his problems. He is obviously a troubled man. He prowls the streets of New York, visiting a sex show, distraught and excited. He wanders, ending up on a ferry, headed out of New York.

Back in Florida, the divorced mother of the three children is seeing someone new, which is why she relies so heavily on her babysitter. She is still young and very attractive, and her relationship takes her frequently to her boyfriend's boat.

George, meanwhile, has begun his odyssey. He is travelling south, but we can only guess where he's headed. When his car breaks down, he goes into a bar and ends up following a young, beautiful woman home. He brutally murders her and steals her car. At the same time in New York, his doctors are arguing about whether or not George should have been released, even with medication. Perhaps he wasn't ready. They're worried and begin to search for him.

George continues his journey south as the mother continues her affair on the boat. The kids arrive home from school and it is only moments before C.J. is into trouble again. He takes the garbage out and sees George watching from across the street. The next thing we know, C.J. is stumbling into his house, covered in blood. His sisters panic and coincidentally, C.J.'s mother calls from the boat to check up on the kids. She hears that C.J. is hurt and rushes home only to discover that C.J. has played another prank. It's ketchup that he's smeared on himself.

The mother, her boyfriend and the two other kids leave C.J. alone in his room as punishment while they go out for a treat. While C.J. is alone, George calls on the phone. Things are getting creepier.

C.J. has been punished, but he is hardly contrite. At the next opportunity he dons a scarey costume a friend has snuck in to him and thoroughly frightens his babysitter. The babysitter quits, telling C.J.'s mother she will never sit with C.J. again. C.J.'s mother is at a loss. Deciding to sell her house and find someplace new to live, she and her boyfriend take pictures of her house for the real estate agent to use. While they're taking the pictures they think they see someone in the house. George is inside, but they don't find him.

The next afternoon, C.J., his mother, her boyfriend and the two girls are on the beach. C.J. sees the man he saw in front of his house when he took out the garbage, George. He tries to alert the rest of his family, but no one believes him. Back at the house, his mother gets an obscene phone call which upsets her a great deal.

George calls his doctor in New York from a motel. He won't tell his doctor anything except that his medication isn't making him any better. Unable to complete the call, George succumbs once again to his nightmare.

The next day, C.J. goes for a ride on his bike. He ends up at an abandoned house where he's arranged to meet a friend. Both his friend and another young girl are murdered in the house by George. Later, the police interrogate C.J. because they know he's been at the house, but C.J. says he doesn't know anything.

The next time C.J. thinks he is home alone, George is actually there. George makes the phone ring and when C.J. answers George warns him to "Leave this house!"

George's doctors finally track him to Florida. They are hot on his trail, but they are already too late to stop the gruesome murders.

C.J.'s mother begs the babysitter to come one last time. There's an important party she must attend with her boyfriend. Very reluctantly, the babysitter agrees. While the mother is at the party, the sitter puts the kids to bed and welcomes her boyfriend in for a lovemaking session. But George is in the house. He kills the boyfriend and the babysitter and then starts up the stairs. When the mother calls from her party, George picks up the phone. She becomes suspicious when no one speaks, but by this time, George has heard the kids. C.J., realizing the danger, finds his mother's gun and when George breaks down the door where C.J. is hiding, he shoots George. He fills him with bullets, but can't stop him. He gets a rifle and continues to shoot. Finally, George falls down the stairs.

As George dies, he relives his nightmare one more time. We find out that the young boy in the nightmare is George and that he killed his father and the woman with him.

In the denouement, C.J.'s mother arrives home. The police show her the body of the man who has killed so many people. She screams. It is her ex-husband, George.

WORLDWIDE SALES
SILVERSTEIN INTERNATIONAL CORP.
200 West 57th Street, New York, N.Y. 10019
Phone:(212) 541-6620 Cable: SILVINTCO Telex: 236747 S.I.C.

UNITED STATES & CANADIAN DISTRIBUTION
21ST CENTURY DISTRIBUTION CORP.
1650 BROADWAY
NEW YORK, N.Y. 10019
Phone:(212) 541-4722

NIGHTMARE press book back.

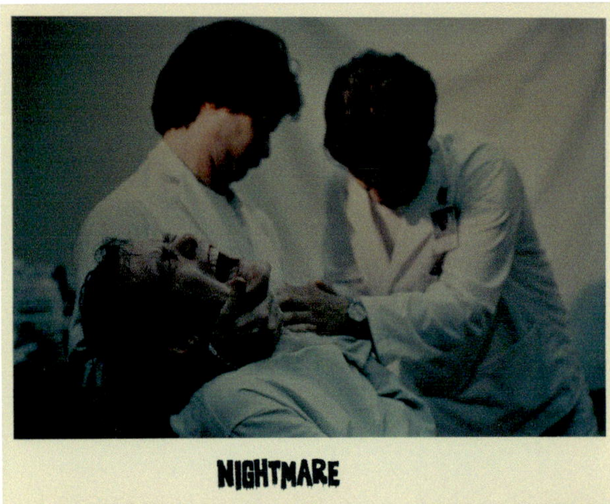

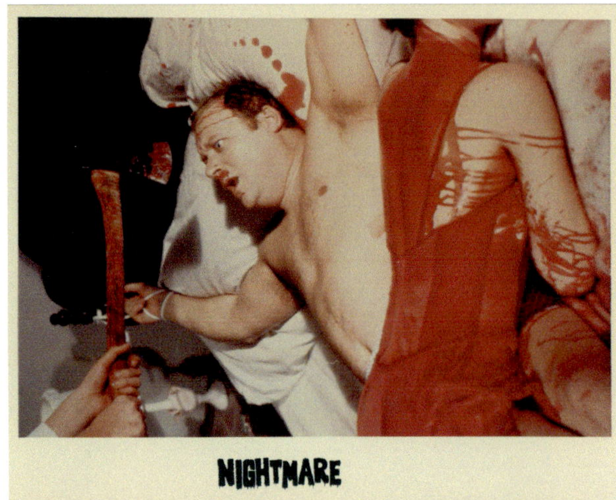

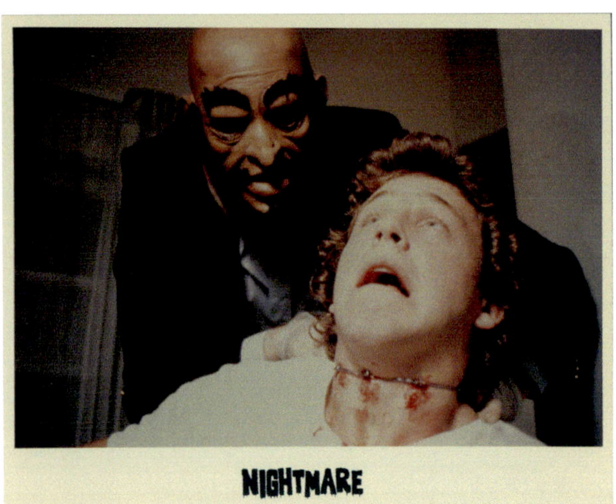

Selection of US stills.

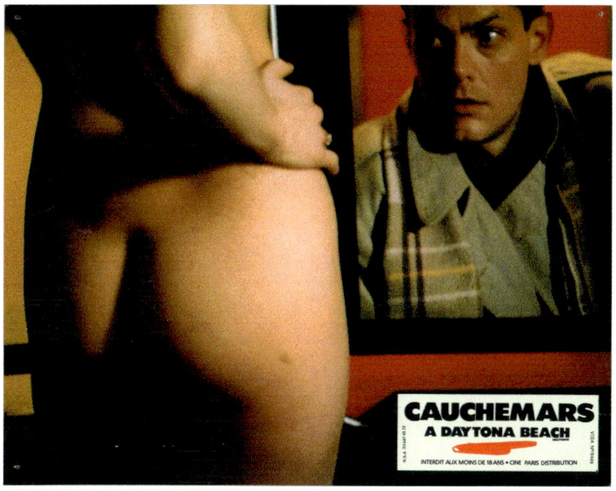

Selection of French stills.

French press book front.

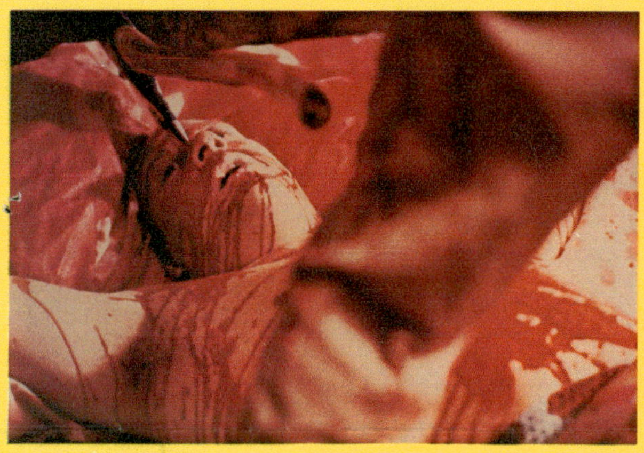

CAUCHEMARS
A DAYTONA BEACH

NIGHTMARE

CAUCHEMARS A DAYTONA BEACH c'est le voyage hallucinant et terrifiant dans l'esprit d'un homme qui devient fou et qui essaye désespérément de lutter contre sa folie. Cette folie prend sa source à partir d'un cauchemar qui le hante ; le meurtre d'un couple à l'aide d'une hache.

Une ville en Floride. Une jeune baby-sitter a la garde de 3 enfants dissipés, ceux-ci se plaignent d'avoir vu une ombre à la fenêtre de leur chambre, quelques secondes plus tard elle est assaillie par un inconnu. La police sur les lieux ne trouve aucun indice.

Un hôpital psychiatrique à New York, nous assistons au cauchemar d'un homme, le meurtre d'un couple par un jeune garçon à l'aide d'une hache. L'homme est inscrit sur les fiches des médecins sous le nom de Georges TATUM, il est soigné intensivement depuis deux ans et l'on expérimente sur lui certaines drogues qui semblent améliorer son état. Il est classé comme : PSYCHOTIQUE/PARANOIA/AMNESIQUE. Contrairement à ce que pense le médecin qui le traite, une des drogues expérimentales qui lui est administrée provoque des effets contraires. Georges TATUM échappe alors totalement à son contrôle et poursuivant une destination inconnue, commence à semer son chemin de meurtres abominables.

Nous revenons en Floride où la mère des 3 enfants essaye de convaincre la baby-sitter qu'elle a été l'objet d'une farce d'un des gosses du quartier. Celle-ci tient à garder la baby-sitter, car une liaison l'éloigne souvent de son domicile.

Les médecins à New York, responsables des actes de Georges TATUM et du traitement qu'ils lui ont fait subir, arrivent à localiser sa destination à l'aide d'ordinateurs. Ils savent aussi maintenant que leur malade est un dangereux psychotique, que les meurtres dont il était soupçonné par la police ont réellement eu lieu, que son cauchemar obsessionnel n'est en fait que le reflet de ses propres meurtres. Mais pourquoi se rend-t-il en Floride ?

De retour en Floride, nous voyons les 3 enfants revenir de l'école, C. J. le jeune garçon remarque un homme sur le trottoir, c'est Georges. Soudain C. J. entre dans la maison, il est couvert de sang et hurle de douleur, les enfants paniqués appellent leur mère qui arrive affolée pour découvrir que C. J. a encore fait une de ses horribles farces en se maculant de ketchup. Nous comprenons alors que l'enfant a une tendance malsaine à faire des farces qui dépassent de beaucoup la norme.

Sa mère soucieuse se confie à son ami, qui lui conseille de vendre la maison et d'essayer de refaire sa vie avec lui et les enfants, dans un autre endroit. Celle-ci approuve et fait le nécessaire pour tout vendre.

Mais le cauchemar se rapproche, on retrouve assassinés deux petits amis de C. J., la police l'interroge, car ils jouaient ensemble, mais C. J. jure ne rien savoir. L'enfant s'enferme dans un mutisme total, car même lorsqu'il ne ment pas, personne ne veut le croire. Il a bien essayé de prévenir sa famille qu'un homme les guette depuis plusieurs jours, mais à quoi bon, on ne le croit plus... Qui est cet homme ?... Que veut-il ?... Pourquoi essaye-t-il de lui parler ?... Quel dénouement horrible va-t-on découvrir ?...

DISTRIBUTION FRANCE

CINÉ PARIS distribution

72, Champs Elysées 75008 PARIS
Tél. : 359 41 33 - 359 21 90

N.S.A impression Tél. 687 45 72

LILLE - G.I.R. Tél. : (20) 57-25-72	LYON - C.O.R.O.D.I.S Tél. : (78) 42-56-88	MARSEILLE - C.O.R.O.D.I.S. Tél. : (91) 62.39.67	BORDEAUX - FRANCE DISTRIBUTION Tél. : (56) 52-86-30

French press book back.

APPENDIX

I. ROCKMARE

Although I had already been a fan of the band, I was thrilled to see a (poorly reproduced) image from NIGHTMARE on the cover of hardcore punk band Jerry's Kids album *Kill Kill Kill*, released in 1989. It was the first time I had ever seen the film referenced outside of horror film circles, and over the years I've noticed some bands have named songs after the film's UK title. To my surprise, most of these songs are more recent. Below is a list, which includes rock, metal, and techno bands. There are some rap and R&B artists that have used "Nightmares in a Damaged Brain" as a song title, but because the lyrics are not about the film, they are not included.

FINAL DREAM "Nightmares in a Damaged Brain" (from the 2002 album *The Future is Dark*)

THE JACK SAINTS "Nightmares in a Damaged Brain" (2005 album *Rock and Roll Saved our Lives … But Now it's Trying to Kiss Us!*)

THE HANGMEN "Nightmares in a Damaged Brain" (2006 album *Cacklefest!*)

THE RAVENOUS "Nightmares in a Damaged Brain" (2008 album Blood *Delerium*)

CLUSTER BUSTER "Nightmares in a Damaged Brain" (2014 album *Total Terror*)

F.K.U. "Nightmares in a Damaged Brain" (2017 album *1981*)

THE SUPERSONIC ARMY "Nightmares in a Damaged Brain" (2018 album *Horror in Paradise*)

LUCIDITY IN THE SKY "Nightmares in a Damaged Brain" (2018 album *Untitled Memory 0001*)

ANGST "Nightmares in a Damaged Brain" (2020 single of the same name)

SAPROGENOUS "Nightmares in a Damaged Brain" (2021 album *Festering in Putrid Spoilage*)

HE WHO WALKS BEHIND THE ROWS "Nightmares in a Damaged Brain" (from the 2021 single of the same name)

II. SCHNECK TO THE RESCUE

Earlier we saw negative reviews of NIGHTMARE, including two published in NYC newspapers. Iin the past ten years, I managed to come across a *positive* review published on the film's release in the Pennsylvania newspaper, the *Morning Call*. Film critic Dale Schneck raved over the film and in his seven (not three!) paragraphs, proclaimed:

"If you're planning to see NIGHTMARE, I suggest that you have a thorough physical before entering the theater. Be sure your heart is strong enough to take the shocks you're in for with this massive assault on your senses.

"The stark, shocking images of a little boy attempting to shoot down the psychopath with a handgun are totally disturbing.

"NIGHTMARE is gory, gut-wrenching, nihilistic filmmaking. It is sure to cause sleepless nights for moviegoers who's most frightening nightmare is the recall of this outrageous new film."

Schneck compared the film to NIGHT OF THE LIVING DEAD and THE TEXAS CHAIN SAW MASSACRE, and (erroneously) praised Tom Savini for the special effects (the Savini controversy wasn't well known outside of horror film circles at the time). The critic seemed to have truly enjoyed and appreciated Scavolini's film, hence finding this review from a respected film critic (and as I eventually discovered, film teacher, producer and screenwriter) was a breath of fresh air.

Dale Schneck's review can be found in its entirety on newspapers.com, and he has imdb.com screenwriting and producer credits for MASKED MUTILATOR (2019) and a TV series titled BLOOD HUNTER: THIRST AND RAGE (2022).

ACKNOWLEDGEMENTS

Much gratitude to David and everyone at Headpress for taking me on a second time. There's no better home for a film book than with publishers who live for and love film.

Thanks to Jerome Reuter, Gary McMahon, Andre Duza, and Philip LoPresti for contributing essays and for their love of the film. I strongly suggest you seek out some of the great fiction and film commentary these gentlemen have been entertaining me with for many years.

It was an honor interviewing Pete Chiarella (aka 42nd Street Pete), who continues to fly the flag for true grindhouse cinema like few others. Seek out his magazine *Grindhouse Resurrection* as well as his books and if you aren't subscribed to his YouTube channel, you're missing out big time.

Endless thanks to Gary Moore, who around 2015 heard I was preparing to write a book about NIGHTMARE, then contacted me to say he knew one of the people who acted in it. After nearly having a heart attack, I gained some composure and this book's interview with actress Kathleen Ferguson was born. Did I mention I love Gary Moore? I'm still dumbfounded how this worked out …

… and hence, thanks to Kathleen Ferguson for taking the time to speak with me at length about her time working on the film as an actress and pretty much in any other way she could. A true scream queen if there ever was one, and a fine humanitarian to boot.

Endless gratitude to Bill Milling for taking the time to speak about his time on the film, and for possibly causing more controversy about the special effects now than there ever were before!

Thanks to Marc Leppla for sharing photos from his incredible collection. I hope you pass those goodies on to someone who will preserve them with as much TLC as you have.

Not only did I get to see Mike Hunchback provide a great introduction for a 2017 screening of NIGHTMARE at the Alamo Drafthouse in Brooklyn NY, but he also wrote 98% of chapter nine on the David Hamilton Grant controversy. Many thanks to this wickedly informative gent. Get in line should he ever announce a book release.

Many thanks to the very busy Michael Gingold for talking with me about his novelization as this book was in its final editing stages.

To all the websites and critics who gave us the OK to feature pieces of their reviews: Venom5 at Cool Ass Cinema, mondo-digital.com, The Spastic Cannibal at Buried.com, Games, Brains & A Head-Banging Life (gbhbl.com), Simon Fitzjohn at movieramblings.com, and the great Alan Jones, who I've been a fan of since I was ten years old.

Lastly, thanks to John Patrick Sterling for the shot of Mike Hunchback's 2017 Alamo Drafthouse intro of NIGHTMARE. Oddly I think it's the rarest picture in this book.

ABOUT THE AUTHOR

NICK CATO is the author of **Suburban Grindhouse: From Staten Island to Times Square and All the Sleaze Between** (Headpress 2019). He has also written two novels and nine novellas, which include the cult favorites **The Last Porno Theater**, **Death Witch**, and **Uptown Death Squad**. His latest novella (co-written with Andre Duza), **At Midnight We Possess the Damned**, will be out by the time you're reading this.

Nick is currently working on his third film book, a look at post-1982 midnight movies and their recent resurgence.